Computer
Systems
Conversion

Other McGraw-Hill Books in Mini and Mainframe Computing

Ranade IBM Series

*For more information about other McGraw-Hill materials,
call 1-800-2-MCGRAW in the United States. In other
countries, call your nearest McGraw-Hill office.*

Computer
Systems
Conversion

CAP GEMINI AMERICA CONSULTANTS

McGraw-Hill Publishing Company
New York St. Louis San Francisco Auckland Bogotá
Caracas Hamburg Lisbon London Madrid Mexico
Milan Montreal New Delhi Oklahoma City
Paris San Juan São Paulo Singapore
Sydney Tokyo Toronto

Library of Congress Cataloging-in-Publication Data

Computer systems conversion.

    1. Computer systems conversion.   I. Cap Gemini America
Consultants.
QA76.9.C68C66 1990   004.1'2   89-12188
ISBN 0-07-009792-5

1234567890   DOC/DOC   8965432109

ISBN 0-07-009792-5

The editor for this book was Theron Shreve, and the production supervisor was
Richard A. Ausburn. It was set in Century Schoolbook by Archetype, Inc.
Printed and bound by R.R. Donnelley & Sons Company.

Contents

Contributors

Ken Berridge

Dave Farber

Ray Franklin

David Hempstead

Frank Murphy

Charles Sirro

Marilyn Slocum

Ron Walker

Larry Wisniewski

Preface

When you think of a book about converting computer systems, what is the first thing likely to come to mind? If you are like most people, you probably want to know what is meant by *computer systems conversion*. Are we talking about swapping your IBM PC/XT for a new and improved Macintosh model? Maybe we mean replacing your homegrown mainframe accounting system with a vendor-supplied package.

Next, you would probably ask why you would want to read a book about this subject. Isn't computer systems conversion just a simple mechanical process that requires brute force and an assertive attitude to accomplish? What's there to learn that's not already known?

First, let's define our subject. This book focuses on the complex conversion projects faced by hundreds of mainframe data centers every year. These large, expensive tasks sometimes require millions of dollars and much anguish to accomplish. Such efforts frequently involve mainframe CPU changes as well as new operating systems and application software programs. Far from merely swapping a PC model or a single application system, we refer to the total change that takes place as a company moves from one computer system technology to another.

Why you should read this book? This book is the first comprehensive study of the business issues involved in a large mainframe conversion. A business manager must consider literally hundreds of details when anticipating and ultimately executing a conversion. More than brute force, we show how and why a business must plan, budget, and manage a successful conversion effort.

Acknowledgments

This book is the result of the combined efforts of many employees of CAP GEMINI AMERICA throughout the United States. The creation and production of this conversion book required a truly cooperative and coordinated undertaking among the more than 2500 professionals located in over 35 metropolitan centers. Along with its parent company, CAP GEMINI AMERICA is the world's largest provider of conversion services. In addition to the actual writers, numerous conversion managers and experts gave their time, knowledge, and expertise. Our special thanks goes to them.

The persons selected to develop the seven chapters of this book represent an elite corps of conversion managers. Most are members of CAP GEMINI AMERICA's National Projects Support Group who possess specialist credentials in conversion planning, methodology, and management, and who assist the company's regional and branch offices. Ken Berridge, the Director of Sales and Marketing for the - Conversion Group, spearheaded the concept and development of the book. The principal writers were Dave Farber, Ray Franklin, David Hempstead, Frank Murphy, Charles Sirro, Marilyn Slocum, Ron Walker, and Larry Wisniewski. CAP GEMINI AMERICA's sincere appreciation goes to all for a job well done.

Computer
Systems
Conversion

The Decision to Convert

When to Consider Conversion

The decision to convert to a new data-processing environment is a serious one for a corporation, one that must be made for solid, corporately inspired reasons linked to the very foundation of a company's business information processing requirements.

Conversion will have a significant impact on all facets of data processing as well as the user community. The typical data center, much like Rome, wasn't built in a day. The existing data-processing environment, regardless of how well it works, was the result of a long, evolutionary process. Change has been consistently occurring, even if it isn't initially obvious.

Most data centers which have been around for a number of years began initially to automate the traditional, manual processes within the enterprise. Usually these processes were laborious and required excessive number-crunching. General ledger, payroll, accounts payable, accounts receivable and other standard business systems generally were the targets of this automation process. The computer systems developed to accomplish these tasks were basically designed to mimic the manual process. Speed was the principle benefit of automating.

Most computer systems developed for this automating process were sequential in design and generally were a form of *batch* processing. Paper documents were manually preprocessed, gathered into a bundle or batch, and submitted to data processing for data entry and computer processing. The data processing department collected all batches, keypunched the data into IBM cards, and ran the appropriate programs to produce reports for the submittor.

In the mid-sixties, when computer automation was just becoming popular, few predeveloped application systems were available. Even as late as the early seventies, vendor-provided application systems were not widely used. Most organizations were not interested in these systems. To some degree, this was due to the cost. The major reason was that they did not operate the way in which the organization processed their data. Computer systems were generally expected to custom fit the enterprise. For this reason, most systems were developed in-house by the data processing department's programmers.

To support this processing environment, data centers required just a few people with different skill sets. Some programmers were needed to develop the systems and provide support for them. Keypunch or data entry operators transcribed the physical documents into a form the computer could read. Computer operators ran the programs necessary to process the work submitted by the user departments. Some sort of coordinating or data control function made sure that all documents and reports were accounted for and delivered to the appropriate destination. A data processing supervisor or manager was appointed to watch over the whole process. The data center was a rather lean organization.

The data processing department was typically an offshoot of accounting, or at least the financial end of the corporation, since most of the processing was performed for the accounting department.

As the enterprise expanded, workloads increased. Other areas of the company began requesting computer systems to aid their departments. The computer became more accepted and less threatening within the corporation. The resulting increase in workload forced the single-shift operation to expand to two and then three shifts and even into the weekend. Processing demands required larger computers, more programs, and additional staff. Computer systems became integrated and new dependencies developed. Users required on-demand access to data stored within the computer and on-line processing became as important as the traditional batch work. Providing expected levels of service to the users became more than just meeting batch turnaround schedules. On-line response time became critical and on-line access availability became essential. To reduce the competition for computer resources between on-line and batch processing, batch work was rescheduled and compressed into non-prime shifts. These new levels of demand required larger computers, different kinds of programs, and additional staff. The entire environment became more complex and difficult to operate and maintain.

As computers became more popular and technology further developed, equipment became less expensive relative to employees' wages. When new functions were required within the data center, existing personnel were expected to absorb the responsibility along with their regular duties. New tasks were assigned on the capability and capacity of individuals. Additional staff could not be justified until functional requirements exceeded the current staff's capacity. For these reasons new functions were not necessarily situated within the proper areas of the data center. It was not unusual to find people who served both as part-time operator and part-time programmer. However, the needs were met and the data center continued to function.

Today's sophisticated data center, regardless of size, evolved from such a scenario. Obviously, this development didn't occur overnight, but gradually over some period of time. And, conversion is simply another step in this evolutionary process.

The word *conversion* has an almost ominous sound. Say it to yourself—CONVERSION—it creates mental images of physical transformation and bodily change. Now close your eyes and imagine a caterpillar wrapping itself in a silky cocoon and then emerging as a butterfly. Change and transformation; moving from one existence to a new, better one; an existence that serves the needs of the host, ensuring life and continuance.

The caterpillar transforms itself into a butterfly so that it can freely roam the pastures of the earth collecting the life-giving essentials of its being. Its new wings sparkle in the sun as it feeds on the bounties of the fields. A transformation ensures the survival of this paltry creature.

When the caterpillar enters the cocoon (after many painstaking hours of construction) it has put itself at tremendous risk. It won't be able to move freely for a number of weeks, making it easy prey. It would be a simple matter to attack and devour the dormant caterpillar during its hibernation.

With so much at risk, why would the caterpillar take the chance? Might it not be safer simply to live its life as a caterpillar? Couldn't it adjust its lifestyle and needs to its earthbound existence? Of course, you know that the lowly caterpillar would soon perish without this transformation. The conversion undergone is essential to its very existence. The risks of not undergoing the conversion outweigh the possible perils of the conversion process itself.

A Conversion Decision is a Business Decision

You may ask yourself what does a caterpillar have to do with a conversion of my data center? Well, nothing really; but there are many similarities in the process the caterpillar goes through to become a butterfly and the process you will go through to convert your data center.

We said that during the caterpillar's transformation it exposes itself to many dangers; in kind, a conversion of your data center will expose your company's data-processing resources to many potential perils.

We also said the caterpillar doesn't transform itself into a butterfly simply because it wants pretty wings; transformation is done because it is essential to the caterpillar's survival. Accordingly, you shouldn't consider a data center conversion just because you would like to be state of the art or because everyone else is doing it. The decision should be linked to very specific business objectives of your company and should not be made for frivolous reasons. The very survival of your company doesn't need to be at risk to make the decision; clearly the rewards that will be realized by your company after the conversion must outweigh the risks and expenses of the process. (See Figure 1.1.)

What are some of the reasons? How do you know if your reasons sufficiently justify a conversion? These are good questions that don't have an easy answer.

In mid-1985, a U.S.-based cosmetic company made the decision to convert from IBM's DOS/VSE environment to IBM's OS/MVS environment. Their justification was simple; sales of the company's cosmetic lines were annually declining because of the growing, healthy condition of the economy. While this may seem like a strange reason for sales to suffer, it had to do with the manner in which the company distributed its products. Cosmetic products were sold by independent beauty consultants through door-to-door and home-party sales. These beauty consultants were for the most part homemakers who worked part-time selling cosmetic products to their friends and

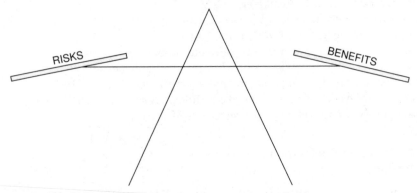

Figure 1.1 Risk/benefit scale. Make certain that the risks of the conversion process don't exceed the realistic potential benefits to your company.

relatives. These beauty consultants worked primarily to add much-needed earnings to the families' budgets during bad economic times.

As the economy changed from a depressed, inflationary condition to a more stable, growing state, these independent beauty consultants would slow down or even stop selling the company's cosmetic products. Moreover when the beauty consultants left, so did their customers; and the independent beauty consultants were the only ones who actually knew who their end customers were. The company dealt strictly with the beauty consultants and had no idea who actually purchased their products. This meant a decrease in sales for the cosmetic company even though the economy was growing.

In a strategic move to save floundering sales, the cosmetic company decided that it was important to identify the actual purchasers of their products. To accomplish this they instructed their almost one million independent beauty consultants to submit the names and addresses of their customers to the company. The cosmetic company planned to enter the more than 50 million customer names on a huge database on their computer. Then they could track the customers as beauty consultants came and went. If a beauty consultant decided to stop selling, the company provided mailings to those customers until a new beauty consultant was assigned. In this way the company survived subsequent changes in the economy.

Manipulating a database with 50 million names and addresses is a sizable project. At the time, the cosmetic company had two large IBM processors in their data center running the DOS/VSE operating system. Traditionally, this configuration provided more horsepower and capabilities than the company needed. Internal accounting and manufacturing were the predominant users of the current computer systems. Growth in these areas was slow and predictable. Suddenly this critical, new data-processing application had to be put in place; an application that would likely consume more computer resources than all of the current applications combined.

Examining the capabilities of the current data-processing environment, management determined that more computer capacity was needed than the current processors and operating systems could provide. The virtual storage partition limitations within the DOS/VSE operating system were insufficient to sort and manipulate the large number of records that would be contained in the database. The speed of the current processor wouldn't make timely access and extraction of the data records possible. A decision was reached to convert the current systems and develop the new application for IBM's state-of-the-art MVS operating system. Only in MVS would there be sufficient capabilities and capacity to provide the functionality necessary for the company's new strategic direction.

Although the conversion project would cost this company several million dollars to complete, it was the only logical business decision that could be reached. Without the conversion, the company's sales may have continued to slide. Conversion in this case was essential to the survival of the company. Any risks associated with the conversion process were insignificant compared to the risks of not implementing the new strategic application.

Let's look at how this company made the decision to convert:

- First the company determined its strategic business objective: To stop the slide of sales by implementing a new marketing program that would allow them to identify, track, and mail to the end customers of their products. It would also permit them to continue selling to these customers in the event the beauty consultant who served them decided to stop selling, thereby ensuring a more steady revenue stream as the economy changed.

- Next they determined the necessary data-processing requirements to implement this plan. These included the addition of a huge database to hold the customer names and the capability to sort and manipulate this data at will.

- Finally they examined their current data-processing environment capabilities to provide these requirements. They discovered that there were limitations in their current environment that would preclude the implementation of this new system.

First the cosmetic company assessed their *business objectives;* then they examined the *technical requirements* necessary to obtain the objectives; and finally they analyzed their current *technical abilities* to provide the requirements. (Figure 1.2 shows an illustration of this process.)

The cosmetic company management probably made the correct decision. They made certain that business incentives drove their decision-making process, not technical incentives. And they measured the risks of the project against the potential rewards to the company. Clearly, the conversion risks were not as great as the risks of not implementing the new strategy. Today their new strategy is fully implemented and their success is represented by their growing sales.

What do you think may have happened if this company's business scenario had been different and they still decided to convert? What if faltering sales were due to an insufficient advertising budget that caused a deficient public awareness of their products? Would management have been correct in undertaking the conversion if business reasons didn't justify it? Draining several million dollars from the

Solution 1	Solution 2	Solution 3	Solution 4	Solution 5
BUSINESS GOALS AND OBJECTIVES				
TECHNICAL REQUIREMENTS				
Extended Networking	Advanced Applications	Device Additions	Operations Procedures	Data Base Technology
Hardware	Hardware	Hardware	Hardware	Hardware
Software	Software	Facilities	Software	Software
Personnel	Personnel	Software	Standards	Standards
Training	Training	Personnel	Personnel	Personnel
			Training	Training

Figure 1.2 Basic decision-making model. From established business goals and objectives, technical requirements are determined which support them. Then, technical solutions are designed to fulfill the requirement. This might include a decision to convert.

struggling company's assets for a conversion could have been disastrous.

Assessing the Risks of Conversion

Don't be fooled into believing that there are no risks associated with the conversion process. Many former information processing officers have stumbled into a data center conversion believing that it was simply another data-processing project. A computer conversion has far-reaching ramifications for your company. Not only will the MIS department be affected by the transition, but the entire organization may feel the impact.

The decision to convert generally originates at the highest levels of a corporation and is done to fulfill some corporate manifest. Associated with the decision, and generally concurrently approved, is an overall game plan and project budget prepared by MIS management. The plans and cost-estimates are usually received by corporate management at face value and are assumed to be the product of hard work and intense research by MIS. Believing and trusting these estimates, corporate management will calculate the impact of the proposed project on the bottom line, weigh the financial impact and potential rewards of the effort, and then either approve or scrap the project.

What's missing from this approval scenario? How about the risk impact that the project itself may have on normal business operations? Most modern companies have become very dependent on the internal information-processing department to operate on a day-to-day basis. In manufacturing companies computers are keeping track of part inventories and instructing robotic machines in the assembly plant. In research hospitals sophisticated laboratory experiments are conducted in computer-controlled settings. Company invoicing, payroll, order entry, shipping, and practically every other common business task has been automated in some way through the use of computer technology.

In some companies an interruption of information flow, even for a short time, can be disastrous. One hour of computer down-time in a major company could cost millions of dollars in lost revenues. Two weeks of continuous down-time could be so catastrophic that a business might be forced to close its doors forever.

A data center conversion, therefore, must be a well-planned undertaking; you can't leave anything to chance. You will likely replace hardware, software, people skills, methods of operation, and everything else that has taken you years to build and perfect. Your internal data center may have become the very heart of the company. Its strengths are your company's strengths; its weakness your company's weakness; its reliability your company's viability.

As the caterpillar painstakingly built its cocoon, a conversion project will be executed with possible great pain and definite great expense to your company. During the project your organization will expose its information-processing department to many perils, which if not properly anticipated, could devour your now-vulnerable environment. Declines in service levels, reductions in system productivity, or even total system collapse are potential risks associated with the process.

Make certain that the risks of the endeavor square with achievable rewards. Make sure that your decision to convert is predicated purely on the absolute business requirements of your company. Then, make sure you know what you are doing before you start. Analyze and plan for every obstacle. Know where the stumbling blocks are, and plan a strategy to avoid them.

Assessing Change

Now that you've considered all of the pros and cons of the conversion decision and made certain that the risks of the effort square solidly with potential rewards, you can be certain that you have made a well-founded decision. Your decision will have been made based on the absolute business needs of your company. It will have taken you through the processes of identifying your company's short- and long-term business objectives, determining the requirements of your data center to fulfill these objectives, and assessing your ability to provide these requirements with your current data-processing environment. If you've reached the conclusion that your current environment doesn't have the proper capabilities, you must discover precisely what changes will be required to provide them.

Changes in your data-processing environment can occur in several degrees, from very minor to total. You must decide how drastically your environment must change to provide the proper capabilities. While conversion to a new environment is certainly an option, it's not the only one. Earlier I discussed the processes of first determining requirements and then assessing your capabilities to provide these requirements. Once you've done this, you will have a good idea of how much change you'll need in your environment.

For instance, suppose one of your requirements was to process an additional 10,000 CICS transactions per day resulting from your company's acquisition of a new manufacturing plant? Upon analysis you discovered that your CPU was running at 80 percent utilization during prime shifts, leaving no capacity to process the transactions during these times. The decision process is complete—you have business justification, technical requirements, and an analysis of your capabilities. It seems clear that you will have to make a change to provide the necessary addition to transaction volumes.

Does this change mean a conversion to a new and more powerful computer model and operating system environment is required? Must you completely uproot your established data center to provide these additional capabilities? You might—but it's possible that there are other solutions that will serve your needs just as well.

What if, after further analysis, you discover that during the second and third operating shifts of your data center the computer becomes almost idle, running at less than 30 percent CPU utilization? Could these CICS transactions be entered during one of these shifts? You also find that it would take about six hours to enter the transactions, leaving you a healthy 8- to 10-hour batch-processing window on the third shift. Maybe you've found an alternative to conversion.

Of course real life isn't necessarily this simple. It might not be possible to schedule the necessary data-entry personnel during the late shifts, or during the second and third shifts the CPU may be so saturated with batch processing that there are absolutely no CPU cycles available. The point is you might be able to switch your workload around in some way that will give you the capabilities and breathing room you need with your current environment. And workload shifting is only one of many possible alternatives that are available to you to extend the life of your data center. There are many other options available, like adding additional memory to your processor or tightening programming and operation efficiencies to make better use of your resources. Just remember, conversion isn't necessarily the only or most appropriate solution to capability problems.

Deciding on a New Data Center Environment

If you've looked at every alternative and come to the conclusion that conversion is the only available avenue, you must decide what you will be converting to. In other words, conversion has become imminent because you've determined your current environment doesn't have the capabilities you require; now you must decide what environment does.

This is a difficult question to answer in any direct, self-assured way. The possibilities for an appropriate conversion target are numerous, and selection must be done based on even more numerous criteria. Technical issues like MIPS (*million instructions per second*) ratings and channel speeds are considerations. But there are usually at least a dozen ways to obtain these with different configurations. What's important is to understand clearly what capabilities you require and what target environments are most suited to provide them.

That sounds simple enough, doesn't it? In our example, using the addition of 10,000 daily CICS transactions, we must find a processor and operating configuration that will provide the needed capacity. IBM, DEC, UNISYS and every other major hardware vendor will be happy to measure the requirements and provide you with a shopping list of alternatives. Hardware vendors are in the business of selling hardware. Their solutions may work. However, you may be subjected to a solution that will require a large hardware investment on your part. This investment may grow over a period of time. It could be that the solution the hardware vendor gives you, in competition with another vendor, is a lowball; that is, the suggested configuration will only sustain you through the conversion and an upgrade will be required in short order. The hardware vendor wins your business because of price, you convert and become tied into the hardware vendor's solution, and then find that you must invest in an upgrade to a more powerful version of the hardware vendor's processor. Be sure that a hardware conversion is completely defined in the early stages to prevent capacity problems immediately following the conversion.

Independent consulting companies are usually able to give you unbiased recommendations. They look out primarily for your interests. Through the use of capacity studies and modeling routines, the independents can design a custom solution to fit your needs.

In general, regardless of where you get your information, a certain amount of technical wizardry must be used to determine what processor and operating configuration will serve your purposes. An evaluation of your known requirements, like the ability to process 10,000 CICS transactions, coupled with the other more subtle nuances like the overhead of a new operating system, must be measured and constructed into a three- to five-year capacity plan. From this plan of required capacity, which accounts for all known requirements of your company, a model can be built which will show the available alternatives.

Remember, when evaluating the various solutions, changing hardware vendors will require more time and effort than simply changing operating systems software. Always look for the simplest possible change to accomplish your goals.

Other, more complex solutions may have a similar appeal to trading in your 15-ft fishing boat with a 75-hp outboard for a 75-ft fishing yacht. The yacht is glamorous and ritzy but you'll soon find that you can't park it in your garage, you'll need a crew of six to sail it, and taxes will kill you. Maybe you should have just upgraded to a 150-hp inboard instead. After all, all you want to do is fish.

Transitioning the People

One certain problem you'll encounter in your efforts to convert your data center is the headache associated with trying to persuade your data-processing staff to make the switch to the new environment. This problem has plagued data center managers since the first conversion was attempted.

Over the years your staff has become very efficient at and comfortable with performing their assigned jobs. They have been doing the same jobs the same way for so long that those jobs have become second nature to them. And if yours is like most shops, you probably have a few folks on staff who have established themselves as the local "hot dogs." They always seem to have a solution for every problem, and you can bet they're proud of the title. If the machine dies or the program won't work, "just call old George, he knows everything."

Suddenly you are asking these individuals to throw away all the years of knowledge and seniority they've accumulated. You are suggesting that they become rookie-trainees in an unknown environment. You might even hire new staff members that are experienced in your chosen environment. From day one these newly-hired people become the resident experts because they know more about your target environment than anyone else. This breeds jealousy and contempt among longtime and newer employees. In some cases the trauma of change can be so great that you may lose some of your finest employees. Employees who understand your company and your applications may choose to abandon you when you need them the most.

What a turmoil! You've made a decision to convert because it's an absolute business necessity. But how can you accomplish it without losing your most valuable employees to the old DOS shop down the street that offers them the opportunity to remain hot dogs?

Your challenge is to provide your employees with sufficient incentives to make them anxious to move with you to the new environment. Many of the same factors that challenge your employees' self-esteem because of their lack of knowledge about the new system can provide you with creative incentives to assure your employees' amiable cooperation. You should, in every way, point out to your staff the opportunities that this conversion offers them personally.

Here's what I mean. If you are taking the trouble to convert, you are probably moving to a newer, more powerful technology than your current system provides. For instance, you may be moving from IBM's DOS operating environment to IBM's MVS operating environment. Because MVS is one of IBM's newest operating systems, a conversion to it means that your staff will gain new knowledge that will be career-enhancing for them personally. Tell them how much more marketable their skills will be as a result of this increased knowledge. If they ever decide to leave your company, they will be able to demand increased salaries because of their new and enhanced skills.

Work closely with your key employees to map out a career growth path for them, showing them how the new environment will offer a wider variety of career opportunities.

Talk to your staff about the training that will be provided for them. Explain how your company is interested in them individually and is willing to spend the required funds to make them efficient in the new environment.

While group discussions of the overall benefits, advantages, and challenges the new environment will provide your staff are important, make certain that you spend one-on-one time with the key employees. This will make them feel like an important part of the team.

If you spend the time to inform and educate your employees on what the decisions are, why they have been made, and assuring them that they are important and fit into the new plans, your staff will make an almost painless transition to your new environment. You will see them standing by your side, bursting with enthusiasm, to help you make the conversion project a success.

Deciding How to Convert

Introduction

The subject of this section is the evaluation and final selection of a conversion method. The decision to convert rests on an assessment of an organization's goals and directions and of the consequent technological requirements. Such a decision is irrevocable when fairly and objectively made. The only alternative to conversion itself lies in a change of those goals and directions. However, the question of exactly how to accomplish this necessary transformation remains an open one. It carries with it the need for as cautious and deliberate consideration as that which led to the original conversion decision. There are a host of issues and alternatives to be considered and their intricate interrelationships prevent a definitive choice in one area without understanding implications for others.

Data center conversions (small or large) are widely viewed with fear and terror. They are sources of stories to frighten the next generation of programmers. Yet they are no more than a fact of life in the evolution of systems and technology. An understanding of conversion alternatives permits you to overcome that terror and to analyze the attendant risks and benefits. In the end, a careful selection of a conversion approach, appropriate to the organizational circumstances and to the technological issues at hand, allows you to manage the very process itself. Above all else the watchword of a conversion should be *no surprises*.

The majority of this section deals with the conversion of the application systems themselves. A clear, detailed definition of the target environment is the only genuinely strategic *technology* decision affecting the conversion.

When attention is focused on the strategic decisions to be made in a conversion, we are quickly drawn to the application arena. There are a number of options available. In the actual execution of a data center conversion these options, or variations of them, may all be used or they may be combined in order to best achieve the aims of a particular conversion. Like snowflakes, no two conversions are ever the same; each is a unique endeavor and during the planning of a conversion choices must be made to properly align the tools and techniques with the effort at hand.

Conversion Techniques

A central issue to be resolved is the conversion technique. Should the operational applications on the source system be gradually migrated to the target system, or should conversion activity take place behind the scenes and then bring forth a finished operational system in one implementation? The gradual approach might be termed a *phased* conversion. Applications are eliminated from the source environment as they are implemented in the target environment. A *big bang* conversion is one in which all applications are implemented on the target system simultaneously. Some middle point may also be arrived at in which certain applications are transferred individually because of their particular natures, while the balance of application systems are implemented as a single unit.

There are advantages and disadvantages to each of these approaches and these should be clearly understood before a decision is reached.

Phased

The phased conversion involves dissecting the source system into units, variously termed *packages, lots,* or *kernels.* This dissection is intended to define groups of programs and data that can be treated as distinct conversion entities, each capable of being independently tested and implemented. All the necessary materials associated with a particular package (documentation, program code, operational instructions, data files, etc.) can then be gathered (in what may truly be a physical package) and delivered to a team of programmers for conversion, testing, and implementation.

Different techniques may be used to subdivide the source system(s) into packages during conversion planning based on the circumstances and the complexity of the conversion itself. Packages might be defined based on file-sharing characteristics in the applications, application system boundaries, job scheduling needs, internal program interactions and dependencies or organizational issues involving end-user schedules, workload, and staff availability. Figure 2.1 provides an example of how subsystems composed of related functional programs are grouped into manageable packages for the conversion.

In one instance involving only an operating system change, packages corresponded to the operational shifts. The initial package was weekend work, for which maximum recovery time would be available should a problem arise. Once that package proved the stability of the system, the next was prime-shift weekday work when the maximum programming support was available to surmount prob-

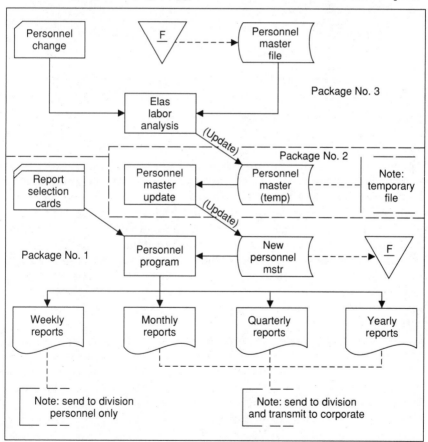

Figure 2.1   Packages as subsets of the entire system.

lems. Second and third shifts were brought over to the new system after operators had rotated through the prime shift for training.

Another consideration in package definition is the possible requirement for *data bridging:* applications, or portions of applications, that have been converted and implemented on the target system must interact with systems that are still operating in the source environment. This may in turn create a demand for the temporary creation and support of mechanisms for transferring current data between the environments. Solutions to such requirements may range from the relatively straightforward sharing of peripheral devices via hardware facilities to the creation of file-transformation programs involving physical and logical data conversion.

A phased conversion is characterized by the stepwise migration of systems (or portions of systems) with some period of coexistent processing activity on the source and target systems. The advantages in such an approach lie in:

1. limitation of risk

2. potentially improved testing

3. additional control over and adaptability of the conversion project schedule.

The most evident advantage is the limitation of risk. If a problem arises in a converted package, then the impact of that problem is likely limited to the particular package at hand. It may have varying degrees of impact on other dependent systems. Ultimately, problems can be circumvented by falling back to the original source system pending repair of defects in the package. It should be noted that this ability may be lost if the package is dependent on hardware or network facilities that cannot be shared or that cannot be switched back to the source system due to demands of other packages. In this case, the general ability to revert to the source system may be lost in a particular conversion, obviating a major advantage of phased conversion. During conversion planning, such points of no return should be clearly identified and the risks associated with them carefully analyzed.

A second advantage is that the definition of the package amounts to the clear definition of testable interfaces. Files passed to and from other packages serve as points at which data can be compared to verify equivalence between the package as it runs on the source and target systems. This presupposes that no changes were made to application architecture or function during the course of package conversion. A profound change in the characteristics of display-terminal screens, or of the underlying file structures, may prevent such ready comparisons of datastreams.

Finally a phased conversion project can be more readily controlled and monitored. Each package represents a very clear and well-defined task. The entire task of conversion has been subdivided into independent work units that can be individually completed and accepted. Should complications arise during the course of the conversion effort, additional personnel can be added with a lessened requirement for knowledge of the global system. Another, less apparent, impact is the improvement in staff morale. Faced with a possibly monumental conversion effort, the staff can nevertheless see tangible, ongoing results without facing the "90 percent of everything is done but nothing is complete" syndrome. Other staff, not directly involved in the conversion, can still participate as they gradually assimilate the new system.

The disadvantages in a phased conversion are twofold. First, changes to programs contained within active packages must be prohibited, if at all possible, and held for later implementation in the target environment. If source system changes cannot be prevented (and, in reality, changes in the business environment may well make such changes mandatory), then that change must be carefully managed and its impact on the conversion project anticipated. Substantive changes, modification of underlying data elements, or architectural changes to the systems may well demand reconversion of completed packages in their entirety or even the beginning of the conversion anew. Lesser changes may require reconversion and retesting of individual programs or the implementation of corresponding changes on the target system. At any rate, adequate change control in both the source and target environments, along with an appropriate communication vehicle between the two, are vital necessities. With this in place, changes will be known and can be managed with the impact of the activity properly assessed and appropriate action taken.

Second, in a phased conversion on a single mainframe, the application systems are in a state of flux with operation of the applications being migrated across to the new system and interim data bridges being implanted and removed. The operations staff will simultaneously operate in the old source environment and the new target environment and must be flexible in responding to the evolving run-time requirements. Such a period is prone to operational errors and requires extraordinary procedures to assure ongoing quality of production results.

Big bang

The alternative technique is the *big bang conversion*. The entities comprising the source system (programs, data files, job control language, etc.) are converted and tested without being immediately implemented as production systems in the target environment. This approach has been described as being somewhat like an extended rehearsal for the actual conversion in which necessary procedures and tools for the conversion are proven, requisite changes are all identified, and skills relating to the new system are acquired. Finally, on the planned cutover date, the entire repertoire of application systems is installed in the target environment as production systems, with all necessary data migration and ancillary changes to procedures, organization, standards, etc., in place.

The aim and advantage of a big bang conversion is to shorten the conversion project by eliminating the redundancy and overhead associated with package-by-package implementation and by reducing planning requirements. A phased conversion implies the decision to independently implement packages in production and brings with it immediate consequences. Big bang eliminates the potential requirements for data bridging and duplicated databases. In the phased approach, target system change control and acceptance procedures must be accommodated for each application package as it moves across. The big bang method requires that these procedures be in place prior to the cutover. Operational requirements may be increased and are more complex in the period when both environments are supported in the phased approach. For the big bang, interim recovery and security procedures become less critical due to the shortened cutover period. In essence, the big bang approach treats the entire data center as a single package to be implemented at once so that many of these concerns are eliminated or minimized.

The characteristic speed of this type of conversion is truly an end in itself, independent of any possible implications for budgets and resource requirements. Any conversion is akin to uprooting and relocating a large family. Once accomplished, everyone quickly settles in to the new surroundings and learns to live and operate in a new environment. The move itself is a time of upheaval in which things may easily be lost or mislaid, normal communications are disrupted, additional expenses are incurred, and opportunities for other activities must be forgone. The risks associated with a sudden conversion must be evaluated against the risks of a phased approach.

The big bang has the advantages of accomplishing the task quickly and moving forward in the target environment. The phased approach allows more control of the target environment and permits growth and modification in a less hectic time frame. Your particular business may dictate one or the other. The important point is to evaluate both methods completely before deciding upon your approach.

Testing Considerations

Testing procedures need to be evaluated differently for each conversion approach. One hope embodied in the big bang approach is that testing can be abbreviated. If packages are entire application systems, then parallel testing at the application level can replace individual package testing. Additionally it may be possible that existing test plans can be reused instead of developing new test plans on a package-by-package basis. The key point in determining whether this hope can truly be achieved is the clear determination of the intent of testing. For a relatively uncomplicated conversion in which automated tools provide a near-totally automated migration, then the real intent of testing is to ensure:

- that no gross errors of omission have occurred,

- that all necessary conversion entities have been transported to the target system, and

- that the application system has been properly integrated into the new environment.

However, for an extremely complicated conversion in which substantial changes have been made in program logic, exhaustive testing is vital. The changes complicate the conversion effort since the difficulty of identifying a problem increases geometrically as the size of the test increases. If available, a third-party application package should be replaced and not converted. If the package is converted, then less assistance can be received from the original developers.

With a big bang conversion, target system databases must be populated at the time of conversion. Data migration facilities must be in place, fully operational, with scheduled allowances made for this step. This is a requirement. The balance of the conversion is fully dependent on this data-transfer process and the verification of its success. The difficulty of this data conversion, not only in technical terms but also in terms of file and database sizes, must be a point in evaluating the significance of this requirement. If the data formats require change or if data is reformatted or restructured or transferred between unlike device types, then the conversion of data is correspondingly more difficult. In this case the reliability of any data-translation tools must be carefully evaluated. The significance of data conversion may, however, be trivial where source and target systems are data- and hardware-compatible, as within a particular manufacturers product line.

The period following a sudden conversion is a period of assimilation since there has been no gradual transition. During this period there will be many ongoing activities. System performance must be stabilized under the full production load, unforeseen operational and scheduling differences must be quickly recognized as consequences of the conversion itself rather than as normal transient problems, application defects must be expected and be resolved in the new environment, and the technical staff must begin to return to full efficiency. The important point is the recognition that post-conversion is a distinct phase of the big bang conversion rather than something outside of the conversion proper. It must be anticipated, planned, and managed as a part of the conversion project.

Conversion Tools

Regardless of the conversion technique to be used (phased or big bang), consideration must be given to the conversion tools that may serve to automate the process. Indeed, the availability or unavailability of conversion automation products may affect the method chosen since the effectiveness of the tools must be taken into account in assessing the risks associated with the conversion itself.

In understanding the nature of conversion technology, the role of automation in such a project must be defined and a clear distinction should be made between *tools* and *workbenches*. The role of automation is now in a state of flux; over the horizon lies expert systems adapted to assist with conversion analysis. At the time of this writing, the purpose of automated conversion products is simply to increase consistency, reduce the risks of oversights, and to reduce labor costs. These products cover a wide spectrum of complexity reflecting different conversion methodologies and different viewpoints on architectural approaches and are available from various vendors and service organizations. The important issue in choosing a method to convert, i.e., big bang or phased, is not to evaluate only the basic philosophies of those methods but also to evaluate the types and capabilities of available conversion products in light of the difficulties and issues involved with the particular conversion at hand. Only then is it possible to balance all of the risks and advantages in order to construct an appropriate conversion solution.

Before discussing specific types of tools or products used in conversion work, it is profitable to investigate architectures for the integration of those tools. This determines how the products appear to the conversion staff and consequently what skills and abilities are required at different times during the conversion. The essential choice lies between creating, setting up, and adapting environments of conversion software products in order to simplify activity during the conversion itself (the intent being to create a foolproof "conversion factory"), and deploying simpler, more adaptive software tool sets for greater flexibility and creativity in the employment of the products during conversion (accepting that staff will have to adapt to the unexpected and handle the unforeseen).

Tools

At one end of the spectrum lie simple, straightforward tools for manipulation of source system entities to yield target entities. Such tools, paradoxically, have their greatest use in the most complex of conversions. These are typically used in combination where several software products are used successively against a given source entity (i.e., the object to be converted, program, procedure, or file); or against output produced by other tools in order to provide the desired result. This tool selection and combination would be subject to either ad hoc needs of the conversion programmer or to a fixed scenario determined during conversion planning.

The advantage to this tool selection, particularly in very complex projects, is that repetitive tasks gain from automation and standardization while the technology remains highly adaptive. A conversion team member can easily intervene, take alternative actions, or handle special cases during the process. This is analogous to providing power tools to a cabinetmaker who remains a craftsperson—an artist—but with long hours of drudgery in the activity of that craft eliminated.

Ordinarily the utility of these tools is further enhanced by providing an interactive, menu-driven shell program that organizes and structures the collection of tools. The conversion programmer can then select and employ the necessary tools regardless of detail differences in requirements for their invocation. A requirement of such an aggregate of tools intended to function together with the appearance of a single entity is that they share the underlying data structures that contain or describe the entities (programs, data, automated or manual procedures, documentation, etc.) that must be converted. Further, this data should be available to the programming staff via common interactive editors, utilities, and simplified program interfaces so it is easy to intervene in the execution of the tools to handle conversion-specific issues and special cases.

Workbenches

At the far end of the spectrum of conversion products lie *conversion workbenches,* software packages intended to entirely automate the conversion process. As presented, these conversion workbenches often bear a striking, but superficial, resemblance to a collection of tools hidden under a "shell" or "umbrella" for presentation to the programmer. A complete conversion workbench represents a fully formed specification of the conversion activity. Adapted to a particular project during setup and installation, the workbench executes the conversion in a far more rigid architecture, with less opportunity for ad hoc intervention.

At the core of a conversion workbench is one or more inventories or dictionaries with structural and relational information regarding the entities to be converted. This is a necessity, since the aim of mechanizing the entire conversion process presupposes that at every step there is available the information necessary to perform many functions. These functions include globally cross-referencing and analyzing conversion activity, indicating external requirements, and intelligently generating jobs and other system requests that are consistent with present and previous conversion activity. This requires that the workbench contain models of both the source and target systems and that in some manner the rules for transformation from one to the other are specified.

Such rules may arise from various sources. A dedicated workbench, created to handle a single pair of source and target environments, may have a body of universal transformation rules embedded within the system's code. Rules may be introduced by program logic inserted at standard exit points or by specification in some macro-type language during adaptation for a particular conversion. It is also accomplished by allowing optional execution of transformation routines based on particular attributes of conversion entities.

The efficacy of a conversion workbench rests on the accuracy and sufficiency of the system models retained, and in the completeness of the rule sets, from whatever source those rules arise. The assessment of these two issues must be made within the context of the particular character and nature of a particular conversion. The more predictable the project, the greater the degree of automation that can be applied in the workbench.

Whichever type of technology is appropriate, the procedural and software technology that is put in place as a conversion environment must be viewed as a comprehensive whole. It must function as an installed set of components and products that act in concert to automate the mechanics of conversion. The necessity for a comprehensive test of this environment is apparent. The benchmark or pilot test ensures that benefits and an anticipated level of automation can be achieved. This test must validate the totality of the environment, including manual procedures, software and automated procedures, tools, documentation, and operational support.

Finally, another category of resource may be required as an

organic part of the project: the human toolsmith. Situations will arise during conversion projects that demand ad hoc intervention with existing procedures or require creation of new tools. This should be recognized as demanding skills outside those normally encountered in application programming, that is, the writing of programs that manipulate programs.

The human hand

Recently the image of system conversions as an independent class of work has been increasingly associated with a software-driven, intensely automated conversion approach. Yet it would be a serious mistake to ignore the oldest, most versatile, and most easily adapted conversion tool: the human hand. In the greater context of a data center conversion that might involve changes to hardware, manual and automated procedures, support structures, organizational structures, distribution of data-processing activities, operating systems, languages, databases, or an unforeseen number of other things, program conversion is one task. Even within the limited context of program conversion, the transformation of a program from one language to another is merely one step among many. To do this requires information gathering, testing, data migration, documentation, and operational restructuring. In a major conversion, seen from that larger perspective, the benefits gained by automating the program conversion activity may be minor. Manual conversion of programs may, indeed, be more sensible.

Undue preoccupation with the mechanical approach to conversion can lead to overlooking the very real possibilities of other approaches. Rewrite, replacement, or redevelopment of application systems must be considered. If the converted system is compared to a third-party application package, then the same evaluation techniques can be used. How well do the functions of the system meet the needs of the organization? How much modification and tailoring will be required? Is there adequate native support (either provided or latent in the architecture) for interfacing with facilities such as a database or network needs? What are the costs for implementation and ongoing operation? What scheduling requirements limit available alternatives? Depending on how these questions are answered, it may be determined that the conversion technique of choice for a particular application is to rewrite, replace or redevelop the associated programs.

Rewrite

The decision to rewrite should be viewed as sheer transliteration of code. This means that all parties to the agreement must understand that the original source system, as it is embodied in the code, represents what will be implemented manually on the target system.

The intent of this approach is to accomplish a very rapid coding project. Programmers can take existing programs and recode using target system facilities, languages, and database interfaces without changing the logic of the system. Advantages are gained in testing by verifying the accuracy through direct comparisons between the old and new systems. This process reduces problem diagnosis time where defects are introduced, and the rewrite can produce high-quality code that can be more readily maintained.

The difficulty lies in resisting a very real temptation to modify the programs for clarity, or to correct perceived problems, or to eliminate minor, irritating restrictions. Since only the logic local to a particular program is inspected and no analysis is done to accurately map the interplay between programs, the implications of such action are entirely unpredictable. This is especially true in old programs well known for violating the principle that systems and their internal logic should be implemented in the least astonishing manner possible.

To the extent that these criteria are not followed, all interested parties must understand and accept the additional costs and risks associated with the decision to modify. The concern here is not whether to make changes; but rather with the clear understanding that if made, those changes will entail a measurable cost, or risk, or both.

Redevelopment

In some cases a true redevelopment effort may be chosen over any sort of conversion process. A vivid example of this is an application created for a hierarchical database being transferred into an environment that will use a relational database. While conversion is sometimes possible, it would be a force-fit of the application and the technology. This is true because execution paths through application systems reflect the navigational paths through their data. With such an enormous mismatch between the logical design of an application and the corresponding data structures, unacceptable, or at best uncomfortable tradeoffs have to be made between program and data design.

Assuming that such a serious consideration is found from the conversion standpoint, several alternatives exist.

- Postpone (using this example) the database conversion and address it separately after data center conversion is complete.

- Accept the unacceptable.

- Emulate, with an attendant cost in performance, the existing data design within the foreign database architecture.

- Evaluate a concurrent redevelopment project, considering added cost and project complexity against potential advantages and profits to the end-user community, and also savings within the data-processing operation based on effective utilization of new technology.

Replacement

Application replacement with some commercially available product may also be evaluated as a possible conversion approach. Presuming that the application serves some justifiable purpose, some expense will be incurred in conversion. Particularly for older applications, replacement (at a marginal increase in conversion cost and complexity) may reap far greater benefits for the end users than the replication of an antiquated system in a new environment.

However, the decision to replace an application may involve factors other than those apparent from viewing the conversion plan. There is the expense associated with purchasing, tailoring, and installing a new application. Added to this are the corresponding activities for migrating old data to the new application, training costs for end-user departments, and the additional costs of dislocation and confusion on top of that already accepted as the price of conversion.

Code Translation

If the application systems to be converted are suitable and fully meet the needs of the organization; if the conversion is motivated by concerns external to the applications, then mechanical translation of the application programs becomes a way to speed the conversion effort. Such translation might be between dialects of the same programming language or from one language to another. In the latter case, the problems of translation are much greater.

When we speak of "translating" program code or programming languages, the very word *translate* carries with it a freight of connotation and meaning. Translation of natural languages relies on metaphors and similes to convey equivalent information rather than relying on precise word-for-word or sentence-for-sentence replacement. Yet even this may fail; the Kxoe language of Africa has no word for any number greater than three; so "fourscore and seven" simply cannot be translated.

The same problems arise when speaking of the translation of programming languages, perhaps to an even greater degree since programming languages do not allow metaphor. The translation of programs suffers from inherent limitations because of the limited structure and lexicon of the languages involved. These limitations raise issues that are both subtle and complexly intertwined, but they must be understood in order to correctly evaluate the feasibility and value of a translation process.

Syntactic conversions

The implementations of a programming language or of alternate versions of the same language often differ in detail due to subtle distinctions in the underlying technology or because of oversights and errors in the implementations themselves. However, handling of these syntactic differences is relatively straightforward since, by definition, they are well defined. Such differences in language may be trivial (for example, rules of indentation) or they may be overwhelming (such as differences in the underlying accuracy of numeric computations); but, given sufficient analysis, they are always unambiguous.

Since implementation differences of this sort can be rigorously specified, the rules for conversion from one syntax to another can be clearly defined. Therefore, the translation itself can be implemented in software. Where substantive differences between two versions of the same language exist to such an extent that a statement has no direct equivalent, the conversion planning must specify a replacement construct. A software translator can then invoke that planned replacement.

Intrinsic functions

Applications are not, however, the closed systems that we like to believe. They come to rely on functions intrinsic to the underlying hardware, software, and procedural environments within which they operate. They may depend in subtle ways on external activity such as operational procedures for task scheduling, or internal system activity such as hardware-level management of data integrity.

The functions intrinsic to the source system environment are beyond the scope of translation. Translation deals with program code and provides a lexical and syntactic mapping from one language to another. The system functions that are wholly external to the application programs and either explicitly or implicitly triggered by application activity are beyond the scope of translation software per se. They still remain a major topic for conversion planning at large.

Equivalence of languages

It may be that application programs must be converted from one language to another. This might be an objective of the conversion in itself. For example, there may be a desire to standardize programming languages in order to utilize staff more effectively; or there may be a corollary requirement because of an absence of vendor support for some particular language.

At any rate translation between dissimilar languages may be, strictly speaking, impossible because of a lack of equivalences between two languages. These differences may be apparent in one language but not in another for manipulation of data at the bit level, or they may be as obscure as simulation by a language compiler and its associated subroutines of unique memory management services.

A central theme in the planning process for a conversion from one language to another is the identification of such usages. It may well be that for one particular application none of the problem statements is used. Another application may depend totally on some source-language feature that has no direct translation in the target language.

Language extensions

A companion issue in translation is the handling of unique extensions to a programming language that are provided by a particular vendor. Such language extensions may be implemented directly in the compilers as new source statements, or as external functions available for invocation by application logic.

Language extensions may provide extended computational abilities beyond those native to the hardware or defined in the source language (e.g., scientific subroutines). They may also be the embodiments of the intrinsic functions described above: source-language provisions for accessing the operating system or hardware facilities not conceived of in the programming language definition. These language extensions, if used, become a source of language-equivalency issues.

Language extensions may be locally provided as well. The staff of a particular installation may have provided subroutines (typically in assembler language) to allow application programs to access system facilities not normally available to programs written in high-level languages. Whatever their source, translation software must allow for these specific differences. Manual effort must be provided for resolution of programmatic differences which cannot be directly translated.

Extralingual constructs

Increasingly, interfaces between applications and other software subsystems (e.g., invocation of teleprocessing services such as IBM's CICS, or data-access languages such as SQL) are implemented with the appearance of source code. Command language sequences are embedded in source programs and processed by precompilers or preprocessors prior to compilation in order to yield blocks of control and parameter information along with source-language statements to invoke the external subsystems.

While these statements are embedded in the source program code, they must be understood to be external to the source language and therefore outside of the scope of translation. Comparable subsystems may exist in the target environment, or may be matters of choice. Considering the possible combinations and permutations of source and target subsystems, translation is needlessly complicated by trying to incorporate handling for these functions.

Efficiency

Finally, in evaluating the practicality of a translation approach, considerations of efficiency cannot be neglected. The interactions of intrinsic system functions, external subsystems, and specific language features may cause a translation to be technically feasible, but the resultant code may be unacceptable based on execution characteristics in the new environment.

Functions provided in different systems seen as equivalent by application systems are generally implemented in entirely different ways. The performance characteristics of an application system are inextricably wed to the particulars of a subsystem implementation either because of clever optimization or by sheer happenstance.

In summary, the mechanical translation of application systems by software tools may be both practical and feasible during a conversion but must be evaluated from a realistic perspective. By its very nature, translation presupposes the existence of unambiguous equivalencies. For some conversions those equivalencies are well known; for others, they are the very substance of the necessary technical analysis during planning.

Once the equivalents (or their absence) have been identified, the applicability of translation software can be clearly evaluated and understood in terms of the effort that can be saved during conversion and the effort that will still be required to resolve program differences outside of the scope of translation. These discrepancies between source and target systems must be understood in general terms but further evaluated as they affect the particular collection of application systems. In the context of a particular conversion, these issues may have no impact; or it may be that enhancement or customization of a translation tool can provide appropriate handling for even those differences.

Code Generation

In some cases program translation is readily seen to be inappropriate. For example, when the functions of a distributed system must be transferred to a centralized environment, sweeping architectural changes are required. Entities have to be combined and consolidated, data must be redistributed, and independent processes must be integrated. The essential feature that characterizes these cases is the rigorous structure inherent in the source systems, due either to the architectural constraints of distributed processing or to a very high-level application development facility that imposes a structure.

The sheer transliteration of programs cannot take into account the fundamental structural changes necessary. In such cases program analysis, with subsequent generation of equivalent systems with architectures appropriate for the changed environmental circumstances, is a more fruitful approach. Traditional translation rests upon an assumption of being able to find standard equivalencies between different, but architecturally similar, systems. In this case a different philosophy is needed. In general terms, the generation of new application systems requires a thorough analysis of the source system with an eye to a precise definition of the target system architecture, requirements, and common facilities. Tools must then be written or adapted to analyze source programs, extract necessary information about processing and structure, and generate target programs according to the defined requirements and architecture.

This approach is a semantic conversion of the application system as opposed to a syntactic conversion of the individual statements comprising the programs. To convert applications in terms of their semantics, i.e., the deeper meaning of the application in terms of the functions and services that are provided to end users, is correspondingly more difficult. It can, however, provide the significant advantage that the result is a viable application system created afresh for the new environment. When source and target architectures are sufficiently different, brute force transfer of an existing structure to the new environment risks creating a host of ongoing problems with performance and maintenance. This is because the system is inappropriate for the technology that surrounds it.

The key for application generation is the analysis of function in the original application system. This generally requires a combination of software technology and human intelligence. It further depends on some essential structural, conceptual, and stylistic integrity in the applications to be converted so that mechanized analysis is feasible. Considered in this way, code generation might be dismissed as a "mechanized rewrite." This would be an unfair simplification. Code generators incorporating libraries of style sheets, templates, and standardized code fragments can quickly and reliably generate programs for the new environment. These programs are architecturally adapted for the new environment, and not blind transcriptions of existing programs. At the same time, program generation techniques can assure the standardization of program structures, naming conventions, interface usage, and improved documentation.

Data Translation

When considering conversions, it is perfectly natural to focus on program conversion. However, data conversion is an equally serious issue. It sometimes produces more intractable problems than those encountered with program code. IBM introduced a limitation of 15 digits on decimal operands on their System 360, where prior systems had allowed unlimited arithmetic operands (you could happily add memory to memory on a 1401). Application systems dependent on numbers with greater than 15 significant digits simply could not easily be replicated on the System 360. The price was providing software arithmetic routines and paying the attendant processing premium. Such problems still exist because of differences in word and operand sizes between manufacturers.

Plans for data translation and population of target databases must be carefully integrated with the conversion plan, especially with regard to any anticipated data bridges. Input data will be converted for testing purposes; output data will be converted in order to compare test results. Production data will be converted and, if bridging is necessary, may be converted in reverse as well. Archive files may require conversion so that future needs for archived data can be satisfied. Throughout, the data conversion process must be highly reliable and well controlled. If low activity data is corrupted, the fault may go undetected for a considerable period of time.

A number of specific issues must be considered from the standpoint of data translation.

Character sets. Character data is commonly encountered in 7-, 8-, and 9-bit ASCII codes; in EBCDIC codes; and, less frequently, in octal and BCD forms.

Collating sequences. Collating sequences for ASCII and EBCDIC are different, and consequently sorted files are ordered differently.

Logic Implications. Program logic may require alteration if it depends upon collating sequence.

Syntax. Data may have, in some restricted sense, a syntactical structure. Delimiters and descriptive information may be embedded within data streams.

Data Access. In order to satisfy differences with the mechanisms for data access, data may have to be restructured.

Management Tools

Other categories of software tools can be used to support the analysis, planning, and management of a conversion project. Some are generic to project management activities, while some are either unique to conversion work or are common functions applied in a slightly different manner.

Inventory

Inventory tools assist in analysis and planning for a conversion. Unless a conversion plan is based on a precise specification and understanding of the entities to be converted, the plan becomes little more than a guideline and the schedules are little more than guesses.

Scanning and counting

There are two forms of scanning software, *lexical* scanners and *parsing* scanners. Lexical scanners examine application source programs (or other streams of text), searching for specified sequences of characters or words delimited in some manner defined by the programming language. These occurrences can then be counted and inventoried. For example, a lexical scanner might scan for the word CALL, thereby counting and inventorying occurrences of program calls.

Lexical scanners require very little setup and can be used to quickly categorize an inventory of programs and count occurrences of chosen code sequences within programs, e.g., lexical scanning (based solely on the occurrence of key words) can quickly establish how many programs out of a complete inventory access a database; and, of those, how many update that database. This sort of scanning normally serves to support general conversion planning along with schedule and cost estimation in which statistical survey information is sufficiently accurate.

Complexity analysis

Parsing scanners provide more sophisticated abilities to recognize words by context and structural association with other program elements, and can therefore assist in analyzing programs for logical complexity. In the above example, a parsing scanner could be set up to pursue the analysis of CALL statements, analyze the succeeding operands of the statement, and record what specific programs are called as well as the structural relationships between programs.

Parsing scanners require more thought, setup, and human intervention but can provide more detailed analysis of the program semantics in return. For example, a parsing scanner could analyze the structure and meaning of database statements in order to provide a model of database usage at the level of individual data elements. This type of scanning lends itself to the detailed analysis of a conversion during which specific solutions are being designed for resolution of problems and differences arising in a conversion.

Cross-referencing

Cross-referencing systems can be driven by scanning software (or can consume scanning inventory information) to produce models of the application systems. Some systems produce hierarchical tree structures that directly reflect the application structure while other produce entity-relationship models. In either event, these models of the applications, internal structures are powerful tools for planning purposes and for understanding the internal dynamics of the applications to managing the conversion process.

Packaging

The process of segregating application systems into groups of programs (packages or lots) representing the units of conversion and implementation can be aided by scanning tools. Additional tools can analyze and organize the inventory and cross-reference information produced by the scanning tools.

Project Management

During the execution phase, management of a mechanized conversion project is most closely akin to management of an assembly line. Staff members use established translation tools and documented manual procedures to transfer programs from the source to the target environment. As with an assembly line, a failure can quickly bring the entire effort to a halt.

Status accounting

The conversion project manager requires tools to continuously monitor the status of packages, programs, and any other entities being converted.

Impact analysis

When a problem arises in a conversion, the conversion manager must be able to quickly evaluate the impact and the effects of the change. The problems can originate from many areas such as an unanticipated problem in an individual program, a fault in a translator, an externally imposed change in priorities, or a need to make changes in the systems being converted.

The application conversion may be intimately related to other schedules for hardware delivery within the overall organization. The impact must be evaluated against product installation, end-user organization changes, and even notification to customers of changes in services and procedures.

The cross-reference system models and the data files produced during scanning and analysis contain information about interpackage and interprogram dependencies with which to evaluate changes.

Scheduling

A conversion is a complex effort demanding controlled execution of a large number of discrete tasks. PC-based project-management packages are particularly appropriate in supporting the initial scheduling, planning, dynamic rescheduling, and reporting the project in light of changes.

Source system changes

Change in the source environment arises from two causes: the detection of program faults that generate a demand for their repair and changing business requirements that mandate supporting application changes. In the first case, the requisite changes must be evaluated to determine whether the effected programs have already been converted. If so, is the change applicable and needed in the target version? A decision is then required to determine whether the program should be reconverted or maintenance activity undertaken in the target version. In the second case, where applications change in order to support new requirements, the effect may range from simply increasing the number of application programs (or systems) to be converted to an extreme of invalidating the conversion efforts already undertaken.

Source-system change control must be created where none exists, or existing methods must be adapted. Change control systems are generally based on notions of audit and QA in which case such a system must also ensure that corresponding change requests are generated to drive the conversion project. That control system, whether manual or automated, must then be integrated with the conversion activity to ensure that changes are accounted for and factored into the conversion plan.

Target system

Changes in the target system must be tracked and managed as well. This may be mandated by strict external requirements for audit of changes, but it is also necessary from the limited standpoint of conversion project management. This control serves several conversion purposes. Changes being made systematically represent an opportunity for additional automation of the conversion effort; problem analysis and program reconversion are both facilitated by careful tracking of changes. Finally, understanding of any substantive changes made for conversion is needed in order to assess the significance and impact of later source-system modifications.

Refresh/recycle

In some cases, where source-system changes are fundamental and pervasive, e.g., redefinition of the paths used by application logic to navigate through a hierarchical database, there is little choice but to scrap the conversion work done to date and to reinitiate the conversion effort. Even in this case the effort involved in reconverting application programs may be reduced if original changes have been tracked and recorded.

Testing Tools

Different classes of software tools exist to support the testing and validation processes of a conversion. Their value and effectiveness must be determined on a case-by-case basis. If the source and target environments are largely compatible and provide substantially similar file organizations and human interfaces, then a substantial amount of testing can be performed by capturing and comparing the file data and the external data streams to or from terminals or other devices. If, on the other hand, files require significant reorganization or reformatting for transfer between the source and target environments, or if external datastreams have different communications interfaces or formats, then such tools for direct data comparison have correspondingly less value.

File comparators

Effective file comparison tools should be able to compare datastreams captured from source and target systems and report exception conditions while making allowance for expected differences, e.g., by providing facilities to mask off date and time fields. Data capture/replay tools are available, or can be readily created to capture data from source system execution and automatically test the application systems after conversion to the target environment.

Test case generators

Software products can analyze source-program code paths and variable usage in order to assist in construction of test cases that will exhaustively exercise the application logic. Test monitors verify the completeness of testing by monitoring execution and measuring the percentage of program code exercised.

On-line testing

On-line testing is automated by intercepting inbound and outbound datastreams. Subsequently, software products can retransmit the datastreams and validate the results. An example is software that captures inbound and outbound data on a PC being used to emulate a terminal; the PC software can then later reenter the data and capture responses for comparison in an unattended mode.

A Confusion of Aims

As the alternatives for conversion unfold and different possibilities are evaluated, it is important to keep a clear vision of the aims of the conversion itself. Conversion is not an end in itself. It is a technological solution to a business problem.

Conversion might be the means of escaping from a technological dead end or it might represent an acquisition of new technologies that better support the organization. As such, a conversion can result in a technological triumph that is a failure in practice where choices are not clearly aligned with objectives. If the aim of a conversion is the improvement of end-user efficiency, then the successful transfer of old applications may result in a failure to meet that aim. The aim of conversion might be to improve programming efficiency by standardizing languages and databases, but if the converted systems are less maintainable by virtue of the conversion process, then the gains may be lost.

One of the difficult tasks of conversion is to avoid being dazzled by the technology or entrapped in the lovely intricacies of the detail/ solution designs. Conversion is often an attempt to eliminate existing problems and constraints; sometimes a brilliant conversion design succeeds in replicating those same problems and constraints in a new environment.

Chapter 3

The Conversion

Project Ownership

Computer systems conversion projects are major endeavors that require flexible yet precise organizations to meet the challenges of migration from existing source environments to newly created target environments. Perhaps no single component of the conversion project warrants the weight and criticality of the notion of *ownership*. Ownership instills the true dimension of the project throughout the MIS organization and the organization of all participating vendors. Ownership commands the full attention of executive management, without which responsibility may be avoided.

Many arguments may be presented regarding the question of who takes ownership of the project. At the very minimum, MIS *must* own the project that has been ultimately approved predicated on business requirements, needs, budgets, timing, etc. However, it is essential that there is equal ownership on the part of all participants, primarily among any outside consulting services that may provide the conversion methodology or expertise and skills to effect the conversion execution. In the absence of ownership by these other concerns, strategic and tactical problems may not be readily resolved. Ownership embraces the acceptance of responsibility, the thoroughness of identifying problems, the challenge of documenting solutions to these problems, the management required to effect the solutions, and the ultimate reward of the successful conversion. Ownership, therefore, may be viewed as the umbrella embracing the many life cycles of the conversion project, from acceptance of the problems to the solution of the problems, and finally the reward of the project's success and implementation.

It is everyone's project, and each group must buy into the endeavor fully; there is no room for faltering degrees of ownership. Each professional organization owns the segment of the project for which they have been commissioned.

Ownership implies commitment, a commitment so strong that it must not be jeopardized. It is imperative to focus on the respective tasks within each organization and ensure that every procedure is followed to meet all components of the project. This sense of commitment warrants dedication—dedication so intense it must not be shuffled or reprioritized to favor events extraneous to the conversion project itself.

Realistic Expectations

Setting realistic expectations is of critical importance in assuring that the project goes smoothly.

Establish scope

Measuring progress demands a myriad of techniques to accurately establish present status for management reporting purposes. To establish a barometer of progress measurement, a baseline reference must be developed. The baseline used for referential integrity may be thought of as the *scope of work*. In addition to a precise definition of the conversion project's goals and objectives, the scope must be agreed to by all participating players. If this is the case, it follows that the scope must be clearly stated wherever and whenever possible.

Establishing the scope of the conversion project serves to shape the project. (see Figure 3.1)

The following describes the basic elements of scope definition:

- *Inventory.* Identification and quantification of all inventory (software and hardware) subject to the conversion.

- *Source environment.* Definition of the source environment including all hardware and software identification.

- *Target environment.* Definition of the target hardware and software environment including hardware definition and descriptions of all software (i.e., operating systems, telecommunications proces-

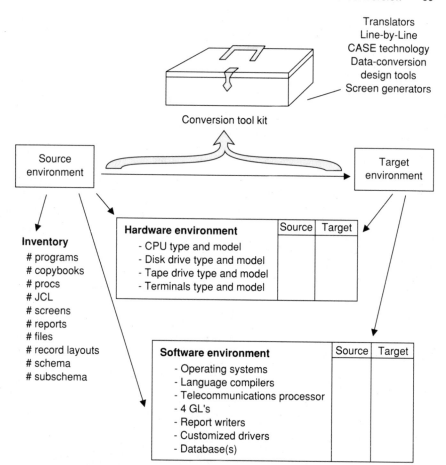

Translators
Line-by-Line
CASE technology
Data-conversion
design tools
Screen generators

Conversion tool kit

Source environment

Target environment

Inventory
programs
copybooks
procs
JCL
screens
reports
files
record layouts
schema
subschema

Hardware environment	Source	Target
- CPU type and model		
- Disk drive type and model		
- Tape drive type and model		
- Terminals type and model		

Software environment	Source	Target
- Operating systems		
- Language compilers		
- Telecommunications processor		
- 4 GL's		
- Report writers		
- Customized drivers		
- Database(s)		

Figure 3.1 Establish scope. Define the source- and target-computing environments and identify the conversion aids that will be employed.

sors, databases, report writers, 4 GLs (4th-Generation Languages), etc.).

- *Conversion methods.* Description of the type(s) of conversion methods to be utilized. This embraces:
  line-by-line translation
  logical rewrites
  reengineering
  package replacement
  database design/implementation

- *Functional equivalence.* It is a generally accepted fact that the vast majority of computer systems' conversions are targeted for functional equivalence, that is, a transparency to the user from the old source environment to the newly targeted environment. However, there are instances where the scope of work will also entail functional changes mandated by the target environment. In this situation, particular care must be exercised in defining the required enhancements.

- *Performance characteristics.* System performance is often a sensitive issue. Prior to any system tuning, general characteristics regarding batch turnaround and user response time (on-line) must be quantified. These factors shape the course of the conversion and provide direction in performance tuning and subsequent testing and performance validations.

- *Assumptions.* Project scope definition may be viewed as a two-step procedure. Step one is listing and identification of all the aforementioned components. Step two lists all the assumptions that have been made, thereby affording the best posture in which to proceed.

Setting goals and deliverables

In the effort to establish realistic expectations once the project scope is defined, a further qualification and quantification of the project goals and deliverables must be published. One way to envision this is to consider the scope definition as the strategic planning phase and the definition of goals and deliverables as the tactical planning phase. It becomes clear that to effect the overall strategy (the scope) we must precisely dissect the project into manageable parcels or units of work.

The goals and deliverables, once identified, are integrated into the master project schedule. The achievement and satisfaction of the total project scope is really an assembly of smaller pieces, intermediary in concept, which once complete begin to form the pieces of the puzzle. Without precise definition of these goals the project becomes unmanageable. Here we have what is referred to as a *milestone deliverable.* Each milestone deliverable needs to be formally accepted before moving forward in the project schedule.

What are these goals and deliverables? Depending upon the size, scope, and composition of a project, the milestone deliverables may differ, yet at the highest level they may be properly viewed as:

Package-by-package life cycle staging

System requirements definitions by package

Project team and task group building

Training

Freeze-control procedures for ongoing development and maintenance

Translation and clean compiles

Testing, user acceptance, and turnover

Once established, the goals and milestone deliverables are tracked throughout the course of the conversion project. Compliance to these deliverables will ensure the timely success of the project. Providing realistic expectations in the establishment of goals and deliverables is critical. Without milestone deliverables, there would be no means of recognizing project status until final completion. In this manner, both successful or faltering projects may be assessed for progress satisfaction and remedial steps may be taken, if necessary, to restore a project to a successful and timely course.

Timeframes, budgets, and resource requirements

As discussed previously, the realistic project expectation is comprised of:

Scope

Goals and deliverables

Time frames, budgets, and resources

Once the strategic and tactical project definitions are complete, the challenging tasks of project scheduling, cost determination, and resource-requirement definition commence. Given the overall scope and the components of the total project deliverable, a deterministic approach to the most efficient time frame must be undertaken.

Timing factors are often imposed by the nature of the organization and department(s) chartered with the conversion project. Time frames may be imposed contingent on manufacturing cycles, processing cycles, seasonal markets, fiscal reporting regulations, machine depreciation and write-offs, or regulatory agency controls. This date (time window) imposition will govern the size of the project and at the same time determine the resource requirements definition. The more compressed the window of time, the more severe the levels of resources required. This is a pragmatic approach that delivers the best *mix* of an aggressive schedule with a reasonable work force factor.

This balancing act must be approached with care. Defining the size and scope of a project on paper may appear at first to be a very uncomplicated "elastic" task. For example, by elongating the project duration, the peak person level loads will reduce accordingly. Correspondingly, should we need to compress the time window, we will face a proportionate increase in staffing resources.

Caution must be exercised however, since the reality of the project does not necessarily subscribe to this elastic effect.

After determining the optimum time frame with the aggregate resource requirements level, these three issues are addressed.

1. They can be accommodated within the physical conversion facility.

2. They can be staffed with people who have the appropriate skills to meet the specific requirements.

3. They satisfy all task-dependency relationships.

If the above issues have been adequately addressed, the cost in commercial terms can be estimated.

These vital components—time frame, resource levels, and commercial considerations—are reviewed with all participants at the earliest stages of the project to secure acceptance and further establish commitment to the realistic expectations of the conversion project. Failure to commit to any one of these components can spell danger during the course of the conversion, and controversy and finger-pointing serve to further delay the progress and ultimate completion of the project.

Corporate Commitment

Corporate commitment embraces executive management's acceptance of responsibility and the dedication and determination to ensure project completion and success. A lackadaisical attitude on a large-scale project, particularly a computer system conversion, will guarantee failure. When the realistic project expectations (scope, goals, milestone deliverables, time frames, cost, resource requirements) are resolved and agreed to, commitment begins. Executive management commitment must continue to support the project daily, not just at the agreement of terms and conditions prior to project kick-off, but throughout the conversion life cycle. Commitment evolves into the daily understanding of the project status, the acceptance of problem definition and identification, the positive attitude of problem resolution and alternatives, and the ongoing balancing act of cost/benefits analysis and risk management.

Without full support and dedicated commitment to the project's every need and demand, timely decisions will not be made. This will stalemate various segments of the conversion project and impede project progress.

When management agrees to the terms and conditions underlying the project and commits support to the project as a mission, they must not close their eyes to contingency factors. This umbrella-type concept of contingency provides the vehicle to respond to both problems and unforeseen tasks that may arise throughout the project life cycle. Having created and accepted the project contingency budget, management can readily support the resolution of those problems impacting project progress.

Human Resources

When executive management formally approves major projects; accepts responsibility for the success of the project; and commits to the terms, conditions, and dedication of resources to the project, a premise has been set that will govern the continuing support and development of the project culture.

Within the infrastructure of large organizations, resource management becomes a major factor requiring special attention and orchestration. It is one thing to commit the human resources (skill sets) to the tasks identified throughout the project; it is yet another to ensure that these resources (people and skills) are protected from other in-house projects, special charters, last-minute steering committees, organizational realignments, and the like. This is why the commitment of human resources is so critical a factor in the timely execution of the project components. Once the skills and numbers of resources are dedicated and committed, management must satisfy these requirements either internally or by going outside for supporting resources. Nonrepetitive, specialized tasks require specialized resources. The careful match of skill to resource requirements is continually evaluated to ensure that planned progress is being made.

During this evaluation it is only natural that changes in resources will be required. Management has to support these changes and see to it that the correct resources are made available in a timely manner.

Corporate commitment to the conversion project envelops the dedication to all the facets of the project as well as the management of the human resources factor.

Risk Assessment

Risk assessment is commonplace terminology in today's corporate arena. Strategic sessions are conducted to identify all risks and subsequently assess the risk factor, a unique number determined at the unit and aggregate level *before* project acceptance and approval. There are many factors that must be considered, evaluated, weighed according to criticality, prioritized, compounded, and ultimately processed in a unique equation to determine a *risk quotient.* This is not a scientific procedure but a creative and subjective approach to a complex matter. The equation changes from company to company and from environment to environment.

In an attempt to offer some guidelines to risk assessment, a list of risk factors is presented. These factors are not a complete list for all projects. Instead they are a representative list of risk factors designed to alert and guide the reader in his or her own risk assessment process.

Risk Factors

The following lists those factors of risk that may be encountered on the conversion project.

Investment cost

Is the projected cost for the conversion project budgeted? What percent of the annual revenue in the data processing department budget is represented by the conversion project? How will the cost of the conversion affect the net operating profit of the company or division?

Return on investment

The corollary to investment cost is the quantification on the return on investment. Does the conversion have to take place? If so, what is the pay back period projected over how many years? Corporate financial planners are generally instrumental in evaluating the return on investment parameters.

Business needs

Perhaps the single most important factor to be considered is the business need to convert. Predicated on a company's recent performance history, is it absolutely necessary to convert computer systems to ensure that the business may continue to function, grow, and generate a profit?

Organizational disruption

What impact will the conversion process have on the organization? Will the disruptions be so great as to jeopardize the ongoing day-to-day business requirements?

New development

Freeze controls must be enforced during the conversion life cycle. All new development supporting the source environment is commonly applied to the target environment in a *postconversion* process. What are the timing implications of this conversion extension? Can the business needs be supported during the *new* development?

Application maintenance

In a similar vein to new development, ongoing system maintenance is a reality that must be dealt with. Can the freeze controls required provide enough discipline and structure to ensure that *all* changes will be made in a timely postconversion manner? Does your organization have the necessary procedures and methods in-house to accurately document and control all changes?

Hardware cost/depreciation

What is the cost of the new hardware compared to the manner in which existing hardware is being recorded for depreciation purposes? Are there investment tax credits? Is the cost of hardware justifiable when compared with the cost of the conversion?

State-of-the-art technology

Does the conversion afford you a state-of-the-art technological target environment? Will this new technology provide a more stable and attractive working environment?

Staffing and availability

The target environment must be staffed with people readily available in the geographical area and having the necessary skills. What is the cost of new resources compared to present-day resource salary averages?

Vendor support

What support is to be expected from the hardware vendor? Is this company local to the area and responsive to your needs? What about the software vendor—will that company support the converted applications (provided they are not home grown)—or will all warranties both explicit and implicit be voided? Do you have the rights to the software to allow for the application conversion?

Technical complexities

Is the conversion feasible from a technical viewpoint? Does the target environment alter the processing functionality of the application, lessening its performance or rendering it useless? Have all the technical issues been properly evaluated (i.e., conversational/pseudo conversational, file and database architectures, flexibility, etc.)?

Performance

Does the target environment guarantee a platform that will either meet or exceed present-day performance characteristics? If not, can performance tuning be effected in a postconversion preimplementation stage? If so, does the hardware manufacturer guarantee performance levels? In fact, what are the precise definitions of performance statistics?

User acceptance

Subtle as well as significant functional changes may be demanded by the target computing system. Will the end user accept these changes after they have been assured of functional equivalence and functional transparency?

Competitive positioning

Will the newly converted system and supporting data-processing environment better the organization's competitive position? If so, how do you quantify the projected gains and efficiencies—and over what period of time will this payback accrue?

Short- vs. long-term solution

Care must be exercised to ensure that not only short-term solutions but, more importantly, long-term solutions are provided for when planning the conversion.

Project Organization

Critical to the success of the conversion project is the organizational structure that shapes, guides, controls, executes, monitors, and evaluates the project. The key factors associated with the organization structure supporting the project are:

1. Communication protocols
2. Steering committee

3. Project liaison

Each is discussed in the sections that follow. Figure 3.2 depicts the organizational structure for a typical conversion project.

Communication protocols

Major conversion projects are represented by a blending of technical and managerial challenges. To demonstrate the success and effectiveness of the conversion project, a project organization must be carefully constructed, providing a hierarchical structure to support the day-to-day demands of the project.

Once the organizational structure is effected, communication protocols and procedures must be documented, published, and respected. Communication is the single most critical factor when considering the multitude of events that transpire throughout the project's life cycle. Without proper communication projects run awry. Once they are out of control and get off track, inefficient and inappropriate protocols preclude any hope of restoring the project to its scheduled course.

The explicit communication protocols that are enforced provide the mechanism for the timely and accurate transfer of information in both upward and downward directions. This protocol compliance ensures that both management and technical leaders are apprised of events as they happen. Proactive is always better than reactive.

Accordingly the communication protocol defines the path of communication required to effectively understand, evaluate, assess, report progress against schedule, and effect problem solutions and resolutions. Communication as a common thread subscribing to the established protocols allows for the timely and efficient undertaking of all project tasks.

The executive steering committee

Earlier discussions focused on corporate commitment and dedication to the success of the project. If a conversion project is significant in magnitude and scope it will attain a high degree of visibility. Because of this high visibility, it is imperative that key decision makers be selected to serve as the executive steering committee. Included are representatives from each major project participant (i.e., owner, hardware vendor, software vendor, consulting services organization, internal accounting auditors, etc.). On a regularly scheduled basis, the executive steering committee meets to be apprised of the project status. Project status includes, but is not limited to, the following:

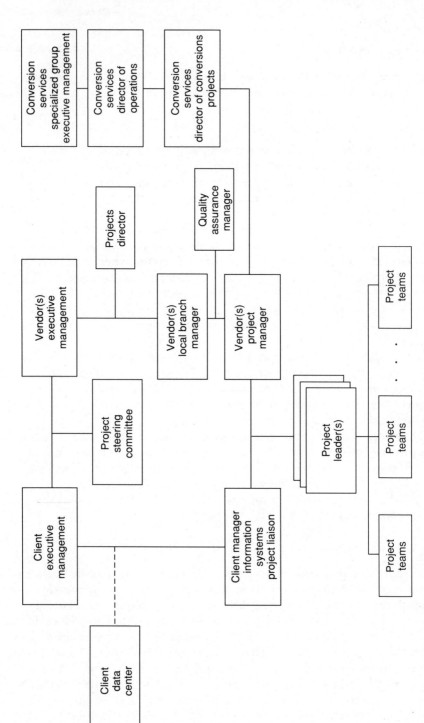

Figure 3.2 Project organization and protocol. Typical organization of a specialized conversion services organization in a responsibility role, servicing a client/customer undertaking a data-processing conversion.

- Original estimates
- Approved scope changes
- Non-approved scope changes
- Problem definition reports
- Revised estimates
- Hours/dollars expended to date
- Forecast to complete hours/dollars
- Completed (100 percent) tasks
- Milestone deliverables (satisfied/unsatisfied)
- Variance (expressed as percent of actual vs. plan)
- Issues and concerns
- Proposed recommendations and solutions
- Next step action items and responsibilities

Once presented with the factual project data, the executive steering committee collectively decides on all corrective actions that need to be implemented and formally stamps its approval. With the highest visibility and the corporate commitments expressed by this group, quick, effective action becomes the project's mainstay. This ensures the most expeditious and efficient solution to bottlenecks that may arise.

Project liaison

While the executive steering committee sits at the top of the project hierarchy, an associated function must be provided for daily so as not to encumber project progress. To fulfil this responsibility in the project structure (see Figure 3.2), the project liaison function is traditionally created. The project liaison is appointed to serve as the focal point for all vendors, service organizations and internal groups. Reporting to the project liaison/coordinator are the project manager, the projects director, and internal project group leaders.

The role of the project liaison/coordinator is defined as follows:

- Serves as day-to-day communication focal point
- Receives project status from project manager(s)
- Receives project status from internal project leaders
- Provides resolution to critical problems and concerns created in the environment (both people and facilities)

- Serves as the liaison to the data-processing operations group
- Reports progress to the chairperson who sits on steering committee
- Evaluates project performance of vendors and internal groups

Solution Development

Solution development exists throughout the entire conversion life cycle. At the highest level, the solution is thought to be the fruition of the conversion project itself. After all, a need was defined: to initiate a conversion project. At this stage, the solution development is the successful replacement of the source environment with a new target environment to solve the business needs and requirements of the organization.

However, solution development is the common thread that not only shapes but drives the conversion execution. The common thread begins in the comprehensive planning phase where solutions to each facet of the conversion are explored. During the planning phase, all complexities in the source environment that will *not* be addressed by the conversion tools and utilities must be thoroughly analyzed to determine the required solution. Examples of these complexities are:

- Programming languages: dissimilar source and target languages (i.e., BASIC → COBOL)
- Database conversion considerations
  Network vs. hierarchical vs. relational
  Flexible vs. inflexible data structures
  Repeating groups
  Data paths
  Centralized vs. distributed database
  Logical and physical database designs
  Database unload/load procedures
  Database consolidation
  Extra segments and stack limitations
- On-line conversion considerations
  Fully conversational vs. pseudo-conversational
  Line-by-line, relational edits → full screen maps
  Forward/reverse scrolling
  CICS restrictions in COBOL II environment
- Data conversion
  Character fields (ASCII → EBCDIC)
  Packed decimal

Floating point to packed decimal
Divide by zero

- Collating sequence—ASCII vs. EBCDIC

- Pause breaks and blank screens

- Function key MACROS

- Real variables converted to fixed-point calculations

- Job-control differences

The solutions to the above complexities are normally published in a conversion workplan document, a by-product of the planning phase. This planning phase is an accumulation of the previous activities described so far in chapters 1 and 2.

Beyond the planning phase, the remainder of the conversion life cycle is generally referred to as the execution phase, comprised of:

- Package preparation

- Translation/clean compile

- Testing (unit and system)

- Maintenance changes/documentation

- Parallel testing

- Implementation

The complexity solutions defined and enumerated in the plan are now employed throughout the execution. However it must be noted that solution development is not limited to that which was documented in the plan. It is inevitable that unforeseen complexities will arise that require immediate solutions. There will also be instances where the defined solutions will not satisfy all occurrences of a particular complexity, necessitating a refinement or redevelopment of the solution.

To further complicate matters there will often be alternative solutions that must be weighed in terms of risk, effort, timeliness, and cost.

Therefore solution development serves as the common thread or umbrella that governs the direction of the entire conversion.

Contingency Planning

General George Patton once proclaimed that ". . .a good plan executed today is better than a perfect plan executed tomorrow." For better or for worse the organization undertaking a conversion project does not usually have the luxury of taking the plan to the "tomorrow-perfect" stage. As such, the conversion plan that is agreed upon is predicated on all research to date in addition to a comprehensive list of published assumptions. Assumptive-type statements may or may not apply during the course of the conversion. Furthermore, there will be daily occurrences that deviate from the planned approach. And there will also be approved or unapproved scope changes that must be integrated into the work effort.

For the above reasons it is only natural to assume that the schedule and budget will be affected. Without a crystal ball to predict the magnitude of these schedule or scope deviations, it is necessary to adapt the policy of contingency planning.

Contingency planning gives a safety valve for the unanticipated. At the conclusion of the planning phase, a detailed schedule and estimate is prepared. It is often desirable to provide for contingencies in the order of 30–50 percent of the original budget. Once done this affords a revised budget that needs to be presented to executive management for approval. The immediate benefit is that resources are provided to address all types of scope changes. In the absence of this 30–50 percent contingency proviso, each scope change will require executive management approval. However, when the contingency planning is approved at the outset, the scope changes become more readily manageable and approval for additional resources is generally not required by executive management.

Project Definition

A project is defined as a finite set of tasks that are interrelated, each contributing to the achievement of a desired end product. All projects have a natural beginning and logical end. Regardless of size or complexity, projects are comprised of:

Schedules

Estimates and coefficients

Assumptions

Milestones

Deliverables

Dependencies

Human resources

Cost factors

Each of the above components will be described in the sections that follow:

Schedules

Identify all tasks that will be required to achieve the desired result. Just as the project has a logical beginning and end, so does each task. The project schedule is comprised of the set of tasks structured end-to-end with dependencies and interrelationships as required. Each task must be estimated in terms of duration (calendar) and then in terms of work effort (resource labor). The network of activities (tasks) that has been estimated gives rise to a dependency network on a CPM (*critical path method*) schedule. Figure 3.3 illustrates an example of a schedule with critical path tasks.

The network provides the schedule of events and identifies those that must finish before the successor activities can start, those that may overlay, and those that have additional lead time prior to start-up. The longest path from project start to project end is appropriately titled the critical path. Those events that lie on the critical path have no float time.

The criteria that enable the development of a realistic plan center on estimates, coefficients, and assumptions. These are described below.

Estimates and coefficients

Coefficients are units of time applied against the number of entities necessary to convert. Depending upon the type and nature of the conversion, the coefficient will vary. Historical data consolidated across projects of similar scope are analyzed to determine the table of coefficients. The associated number of entities to be converted or processed are determined via sophisticated scanning software that is employed during the planning phase. The extension of the number of entities multiplied by the desired coefficient begins to build the task effort. Add to that the setup time, the rework time (manual), and the management required and we arrive at the effort estimate for a given activity.

The estimate is only as good as the validity of the coefficients and the accuracy of the entity counts.

Assumptions

Assumptions need to be documented in full detail during the planning, estimating, and schedule development. The assumptions drive the entire planning/schedule phase. In the absence of assumptions, all subsequent progress monitoring and checks and balances will not have the appropriate baseline by which to be gauged. Therefore it is essential that *all* assumptions be documented and published. Future

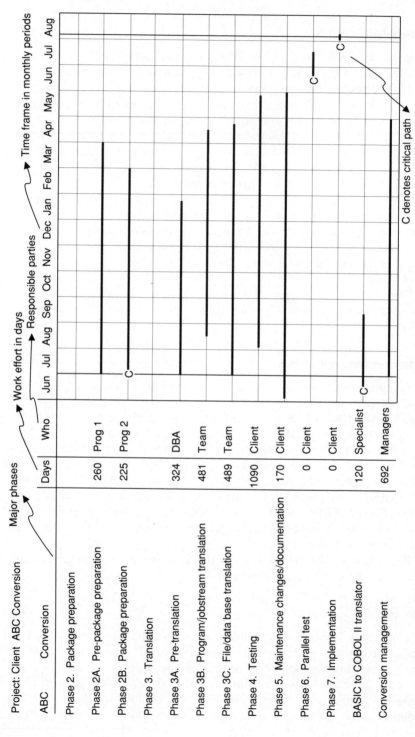

Figure 3.3 Project schedule. High-level major-phase definition displays phases, work effort in days, responsibility for each phase ("who"), and relative calendar timeline durations.

variances (actual vs. plan) may then be evaluated in light of the assumption. If the assumption proves to be correct then the variances are due to either increased or decreased performance. If the assumptions governing a particular task or set of tasks are no longer valid, then the variances are adjusted accordingly.

The documentation of assumptions provides the baseline for rational decision making, which contributes to the development of more realistic schedules.

Milestones

During the development of the project schedules the number of project tasks may grow enormously (2–3 thousand activities on a large-scale project is not uncommon). The project must then be dissected into critical phases. Each critical phase must have a milestone associated with it. Once the milestones are identified, progress measurement is more readily effected by evaluating the achievement of the milestones. A milestone is not a task. Actually the milestone should represent a targeted moment when a series or group of activities are scheduled for completion.

The tracking of milestone achievement provides a higher level of progress status.

Deliverables

While milestones represent a point in time when a series of activities are scheduled for completion, deliverables represent more tangible criteria used in determining progress status and measurement. Each item on the activity list is associated with a particular deliverable. The basic characteristic of a deliverable is that it is a manageable and measurable parcel of work. It is either done or not done—partial completions are not meaningful. This is why the precise enumeration of all required tasks/deliverables is essential for a realistic and manageable schedule.

Dependencies

There are four types of task interrelationships:

- Finish-to-start
- Finish-to-finish
- Overlap
- Lag

Each of these four dependency types allows the structuring of the project network. There are activities that require the completion of preceding (predecessor) activities before the successor can even begin. These are classified as *finish-to-start*. *Finish-to-finish* activities are those that have varying start times but must be completed at the same point in time. *Overlap* activities are those that may start after its predecessor gets underway. Finally, *lag* activities are those that need to begin after a specified period of time after the predecessor activity ends.

The use of these dependencies allows ongoing what-if analyses to occur. All events that are not on schedule (either ahead or behind) are evaluated and the critical path scheduling techniques will analyze all the ramifications of the schedule predicated on current progress. This thorough schedule analysis quickly identifies revised end dates as well as newly created resource constraints. This procedure allows the project manager to be in a proactive, rather than reactive, position.

Human resources

In addition to the identification of effort estimates for all activities, it is also a requirement to identify the appropriate resources associated with the particular activity. Resources are comprised of people, hardware, software, services, and dollars.

Generally speaking we can focus on the human resources, as they constitute the majority of the resource requirements in a major data-processing conversion project.

The allocation of specific resources to the tasks results in a projected demand on each resource. A tendency exists to overcommit employees. The resource aggregation procedure available within the CPM software packages clearly indicates the underloads and overloads. Once these erratic peaks and valleys are indicated for each resource, the process of resource leveling is applied. This is a heuristic approach that attempts to reschedule all noncritical activities (i.e., those having some inherent float-slack time) in order that peaks are reshuffled into the valleys. The heuristic leveling therefore smooths the human resources curve, contributing to a more manageable project. Figure 3.4 illustrates the leveling of worker resources.

Cost factors

Cost can be introduced into the project schedule in two manners.

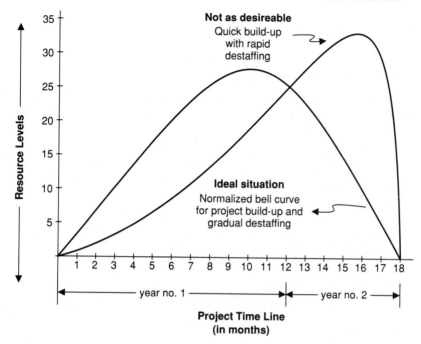

Figure 3.4 Staffing levels. Both the black and red staffing-level curves illustrate a gradual buildup of resources and subsequent destaffing. The red-coded curves more closely approximates a normalized bell curve that provides better management of the staff resources.

1. Fixed costs

2. Variable costs—resources

Fixed costs are applied directly against a task (i.e., a task to acquire a software package or utility is costed at $50,000). Variable costs are directly associated with the resource(s) applied to the activity (i.e., hourly or daily billing rate). These costs are extended according to the level of effort identified across each task. By encoding each task, the costs may be presented by:

Resource

Vendor

Skill category

Task category

Costs are further presented in report formats often highlighting:

Actual-to-date costs

Forecast-to-complete costs

Latest cost-estimates

Original cost-estimate

Cost variance

This information is invaluable to the project manager chartered with the responsibility of a quality conversion within time and budget constraints.

Tracking and Monitoring

Beyond developing a project plan, the project manager must also control and manage the course of the conversion project. The process of project tracking requires periodic assessment of project status, namely, what the actual progress is compared to plan. Two major areas to consider are:

1. Schedule reassessment
2. Project impact analysis

Schedule reassessment

Periodically the project schedule must be assessed to determine progress against plan. Project tracking is the forerunner to this effort. Tracking requires the timely posting of work effort against tasks. This is achieved by either marking tasks complete or posting time worked against each scheduled task. Similarly, it is essential that the responsible resource for each task forecasts the time remaining to complete the task. Often the forecasted time remaining will differ from the calculated remaining time (original estimate minus time-to-date). This is necessary to determine the revised estimate that, when compared with the original estimate, yields a variance.

At the time of updating the schedule, latest start and finish dates may also change, and this data must be entered into the project schedule. Figure 3.5 shows the variance that may occur between the originally scheduled hours, the hours actually worked, and those earned (based only on tasks fully completed). With the posting of this timely update data, the project manager must assess the new schedule, noting slippage and resource over- or underloads. Project rescheduling is performed to restore the project to its original course.

Project impact analysis

Project impact analysis is required to report all events that impact the project schedule or project cost at the time they occur. Project impacts may be classified into three general categories:

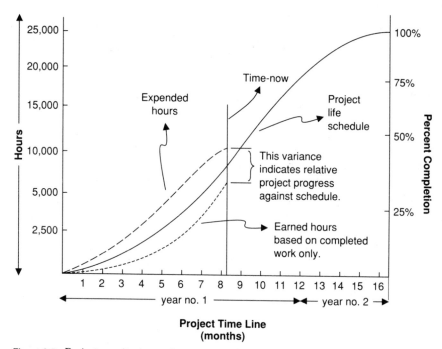

Figure 3.5 Project monitoring and status reporting. The current overview of the project (time-now) illustrates the scheduled hours (—— solid line), the actual hours (— — — broad dash line), and the earned hours (- - - - broken line).

1. Scope change
2. Lost time
3. Other

Once the impact is noted, research must determine the impact, usually defined by hours/cost/delay. This is an iterative process determined by updating the project schedule and performing "what if" analysis using the critical path method (CPM) of scheduling. A complete breakdown of the impact estimate should be presented to the executive management for formal approval. It is only through the formal approval cycle that the impact may be identified in the project schedule and subsequently worked on.

There are often cost/benefit analyses that must be considered before authorizing the scope changes. A common scope change may indicate that the project end date may slip n weeks. The cost of this slippage must then be weighed against the cost of introducing additional resources to reduce the slippage.

The formal approval cycle cited above results in both approved and unapproved scope changes. It is sound project management practice to introduce each of these type changes categorically into the project control system. This allows project management to report on project status, both inclusive and exclusive of these scope changes.

Problem identification and resolution

During regularly scheduled project-status meetings a forum is established to review current progress, planned activities and problems and concerns. The problem-identification segment requires open disclosure related to the nature of the problem, i.e., when it occurred, the reasons that it occurred, who is responsible for its occurrence, and most importantly, what solutions have been proposed to remedy the situation. It is important that project management not only cite the problem and its impact, but also be properly prepared to discuss possible solutions.

After the review of the problem and its causes, the project steering committee must be informed of the ramifications of the problem. The most common problems often manifest themselves in:

- Project delays
- Revised project end date(s)
- Non-efficient utilization of project resources
- Unanticipated costs (covered by contingency planning)
- Bad morale
- Lost project momentum

Solving the problem at hand clearly prevents a host of future problems. Analyzing and evaluating the proposed solutions is a joint effort between the customer and outside vendors. All members on the steering committee must carefully weigh the benefits/risks quotient to determine the optimum solution.

After agreement has been reached on the problem's solution, the project management team must introduce the solution tasks, durations, responsibilities, and interfaces into the current project master schedule. This effort must not be taken lightly—any impacts on project schedule have both near-term and far-reaching ramifications.

Mobilizing outside resources

Outside resources may be required at varying stages of the conversion project. These resources may be requested for a number of different reasons in each project environment. Some reasons are presented below:

- Staff limitations
- Expertise not available in-house
- Project management expertise
- Timely availability and responsiveness
- Corporate auditor's recommendation
- Solution packaging

Typically in a major computer systems conversion project, outside resources will be contracted to provide the complete solution—from planning through conversion execution through final parallel and implementation—working closely with the project management although responsibility is awarded to the service organization. This approach significantly reduces the risk inherent in a conversion that is attempted without the customer's proven expertise and practicality.

Planning for Quality

In previous sections we discussed some of the key components researched and identified in the planning phase. After the analytical and fact-finding efforts have been completed, the task of project-schedule development commences. Inherent in the design and structuring of the conversion master schedule are the underlying quality parameters that must also be considered. Not only is it necessary to identify, estimate, and schedule all finite tasks that constitute the project execution phase, it is also essential to define the process that will ensure that all deliverables will meet expectations. A quality plan must address all of the managerial, procedural, technical, and organizational measures that are to be utilized through the project life cycle to ensure the quality deliverable in final form. To build quality into the project requires the precise definition of:

- Project goals
- Project responsibilities
- Project technical guide
- Project plans
- Deliverable quality-assurance audits
- Management control

Perhaps no one single component contributes to the overall quality as a project technical guide does. This document describes the environment in which the project deliverables are produced. However, even more importantly it describes the:

- Standards
- Conventions
- Procedures
- Protocols
- Methods
- Techniques
- Tools

that are required to meet all deliverables. It is this document that is adapted as the standard to ensure high quality built into the master plan, and is accepted by the client as the vehicle to drive project compliance.

When to be involved

In the real estate market, a claim is made that "location, location, location" are the three most important aspects of a successful investment. In major projects, the adage may read "involvement, involvement, involvement" as the critical factor in the success of the conversion project.

Involvement from executive management must be associated in, but not limited to, the following phases:

- During the start-up stage
- Project manager start-up meetings
- Project users/task group start-up meetings
- During the execution stage
- Periodic status meetings
- Problem-identification sessions
- Problem-resolution meetings
- Executive steering committee meetings
- Quality-assurance audits
- Functional deliverable sessions
- During the wrap-up stage
- Final parallel
- Final implementation
- Formal deliverable sign-offs

An all-important involvement on a day-to-day basis is required to communicate information in a timely manner. This allows the decision-making effort to be based on accuracy and criticality, not on simply a crisis basis.

Two of the major reasons for project failure in any environment or industry are lack of interest and noninvolvement. Not being involved is akin to not being committed. Lack of commitment breaks the foundation upon which the project success is built. You must be involved at all times. All subcontractors (vendors) must also be involved during each critical project phase.

Change management

Change management is one of the phases contained in the conversion life cycle. During the course of the conversion, it is only natural that the source environment progresses to support operational changes, program modification, and system enhancements. There are few instances where a stop may be imposed on the ever-evolving data center.

Therefore, in an attempt to allow the data center operation to evolve while in a parallel mode, the conversion demands very stringent change control measures and procedures.

A formal control-and-change management procedure is required to document all changes and provide contractors with complete information concerning these changes, modifications, or enhancements. Specifically, information must be captured describing the change, the system(s) affected by the change, and the timing and effort associated with implementing the change.

The impact of the changes (which also includes scope changes as defined during the conversion execution phase) must be measured accordingly. These measures are listed below:

- Get management approval for the research.

- Add the approved research to a log of newly added work.

- Evaluate the impact of the approved research work to the master project schedule.

- Determine the impact on the master schedule in terms of hours, cost, resources, impacted milestones, and end dates.

- Secure management and executive steering committee approval for the scope changes.

- Introduce the work requirements to the master schedule, reschedule, and present revised milestone and target end dates.

Changes not classified as approved scope changes must be implemented in a postconversion manner so as not to disrupt or impede progress.

Compliance

Project compliance in fulfilling formal requirements strengthens the ability to progress in an orderly, scheduled manner. The formal requirements are defined during the course of project responsibility definition. This describes the resource(s) responsible for the assigned tasks on the project. Properly describing the entire host of project responsibilities clarifies required commitments prior to the inception of the project plan and execution.

Compliance ensures meeting scheduled progress while addressing and resolving all circumstances that may negatively impact the project. In the absence of compliance the success of the project is severely hampered.

4

Organization—Addressing the Changing Environment

Project Team Orientation

As with any project, and in particular a conversion project, it is necessary to have a project team consisting of many talented people dedicated to the endeavor. To be successful, this team must fully comprehend its mission both as a group and as individuals. To this end team members must be oriented to the project as a whole, have their roles and responsibilities defined, and have a complete understanding of the different relationships within the corporate infrastructure.

Project team orientation is a key factor in the success or failure of any project. Generally conducted by the project manager at the onset of the project or as new members are added, orientation consists of six major areas (see Figure 4.1):

1. Reasons behind the conversion
2. Project scope, goals, and deliverables
3. Standards and procedures
4. Performance criteria
5. Roles and responsibilities
6. Corporate infrastructure relationships

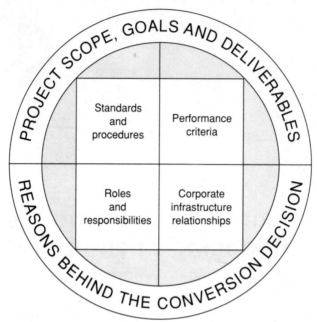

Figure 4.1 Orientation: a means for everyone to set their sights properly.

The latter two areas were discussed in detail in the preceding sections.

In discussing the reasons behind the conversion, team members become familiar with the business perspectives of the decision. Additionally they gain any knowledge of the pitfalls or key functional areas of the systems that are to be converted. This gives members of the team a solid foundation upon which to build their understanding of the project that lies before them.

The next and critical part of the orientation process is the clear and concise definition of project scope, goals, and deliverables. It is of paramount importance that all members understand and agree upon these three items. This will ensure that all team members comprehend what the project is to achieve and what the resulting outcomes should be. More often than not it is a lack of understanding of these objectives that produces a project doomed to failure.

The entire project team must know where they are going and why, and it is important to set guidelines for how the work is to be accomplished. This is where standards and procedures come into play. The standards and procedures reflect not only the rules to be followed for recreating the old system or systems in the target environment (such as JCL standards, coding procedures, and document requirements), but also the rules governing the project team itself. These can include working hours, problem-resolution procedures, reporting procedures, and project tracking procedures.

Another crucial part of the orientation process is the team's understanding of the overall performance criteria. It is important from a motivational standpoint that all team members are able to measure not only their own effectiveness but the productivity and performance of the team as a whole against tasks and major milestones. It must be understood by all team members that performance criteria is the means by which corporate management is able to determine exactly how the project is progressing.

The roles and responsibilities of the team members as well as the relationships that exist within the corporate infrastructure are the final items covered in the orientation. Both topics will be discussed in more detail in the following subsections.

Roles and Responsibilities

An important part of any job is understanding one's role within the organization and its associated responsibilities. The same is true within the context of a conversion project team. The decision of which members will perform specific tasks is the project manager's and it is communicated to the individuals or groups during the orientation process.

Skill-level assessment

In first determining the tasks to be assigned to individuals or groups, make an assessment of the skills and knowledge base the project team members bring to the organization. This is not a simple task and demands time not only from the project manager but the direct superiors of the project team members and personnel department as well and includes the possibility of interviewing the team members themselves before the project begins. The assessment must take into account not only the current technical skills of the individual but any past training or experience that would be relevant to the conversion project. Equally important is the individual's level of managerial expertise and how well the person deals with others inside a group and with people who must interface with the group.

The simplest method for determining this kind of information is to review each team member's resumé and discuss current performance and skill levels with the individual's current superior. Although this is the quickest method for determining someone's skill set, it is not necessarily the entire picture. It is highly advisable to interview each individual and make an assessment from all the facts.

Care must be taken to enlist individuals who not only possess the correct skills but also the correct attitude and ability to deal with others. This process should not be made into "superstar" search but should focus on recruiting the best possible people for the job. It is wise to remember the adage "the whole should be greater than the sum of its parts" when deciding on the people to be involved in a project.

Once all individuals comprising the conversion project team have been assessed, decide on both the interpersonal makeup that will benefit the team when broken into groups and the skill requirements that must be present to fulfill the specific tasks of the project. Then and only then can specific tasks be delegated to the individuals.

Task-specific assignments

After the analysis of the skills of individuals on the project has been successfully completed, it must be decided which tasks are best suited for each individual. Although certain tasks such as coding are considered grouped, this is not sufficient. Tasks must be broken down into specific and measurable items so that definite goals and time frames may be defined. This results in specific criteria for the achievement of the task being well-defined. Certain tasks might involve a high degree of user interface while others might have none. Still other tasks might require a technical skill level far beyond the norm. The job of matching these criteria to the available resources is one of the more difficult duties since it is judgment alone that will determine which person is best suited to perform a particular task. In addition it is necessary to decide if that person will be able to complete the specific task within the time constraint of the schedule. The completion of this task may impact the beginning of the next task that this person is assigned.

Depending on the size of the conversion there will also be the need for the assignment of intermediate managers. These intermediate managers will be responsible for the completion of functionally or logically grouped sets of tasks as well as the people who have been assigned to complete these tasks. These intermediate managers and their subordinates must be chosen carefully so that conflicts in personality do not arise. The sign of a good manager is the ability to pick and nurture other individuals who have the potential to become managers as well as the necessary interpersonal skills required to control or avoid conflict.

It is during the project team orientation that the roles and responsibilities for each individual within the team is laid out. It is of extreme importance to have both the understanding and the explicit agreement of all members as to the roles they will play during the conversion, the tasks that they have been assigned, and how they are all key to the successful completion of the project. The project team must be made aware that it is not the project manager's sole responsibility to implement the conversion. The project in and of itself is of vital importance to the organization as a whole. Thus the project is the responsibility of all individuals, whether they are directly related to the project or not.

Corporate Infrastructure Relationships

Within the context of any organization there are levels of hierarchy. For a conversion project team there is the internal hierarchy which is defined by the above-mentioned roles and responsibilities, the external hierarchies, the sponsoring organization or steering committee, and the remainder of the organization or user community. It is ultimately the sponsoring organization and the user community that the project team will endeavor to satisfy. In addition to these hierarchies, there is also an informal structure that exists for emergency or crisis situations. Although it is everyone's hope that this organization does not have to be used, it is an everyday fact that sooner or later a major crisis will arise.

Reporting lines

To be able to determine progress and resolve issues both within the project team itself and outside the team, definite lines of communication or reporting lines must be established, known, and most importantly of all, utilized. A conversion project cannot stand apart from its human resources. You must be kept abreast of the status of each of the tasks within the project. The steering committee must be kept aware of project progress. They are also responsible for solving problems that cannot be solved by the project team. These problems are brought to the steering committee's attention so that an expedient solution can be found. Finally, the user community must be kept up-to-date on the development of the systems that they are dependent upon.

A conversion project involves many people with varying interests. It is important that the information each group desires is delivered in a concise, uniform, and timely fashion. To achieve this and prevent chaos, the reporting structure between groups should be kept to the bare minimum and adhered to at all costs. This will prevent many different versions of the same story from occurring or, worse yet, misinterpretation of the original story. The sample reporting structure chart (see Figure 4.2) shows a simplistic, yet realistic, view of the reporting lines that should be established during a conversion project.

The diagram illustrates that a single interface for each of the parties involved makes for an easier transfer of information and coordination of tasks to be accomplished.

Crisis management

One of the most tangible structures in any organization is the one that deals with crisis situations. No two crises are the same and all are of different magnitude from project to project and company to company. In all cases crisis management calls for cool heads and strong decisions. The key is by whom and when.

Within a conversion project crises may take on different forms but the end factor is the same. Resources must be diverted from one activity to the problem at hand. Within the confines of the conversion project itself one must make the key decision as to which people

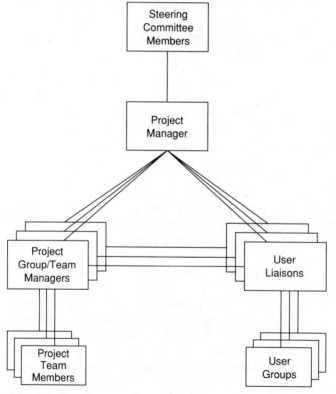

Figure 4.2 Sample conversion-project reporting lines.

will be diverted from their current tasks to resolve the problem. This is done with a full knowledge of where there is slack time or where the resulting impact will occur. The decision is not made in conjunction with any subordinate managers although they must live with the decision and its consequences. When a situation demands more resources than are available within the project, a single point of contact is needed to allow mobilization of resources external to the project as quickly as possible. This is generally the data processing director or someone of equivalent status who sits on the steering committee.

The key to the process is not reduced management involvement but full management awareness. Even in the reverse situation, where resources dedicated to the conversion project are needed to resolve a crisis outside of the project, it may sometimes be necessary to relinquish the necessary resources.

It is important for any organization to be structured in a manner that allows flexibility. The resulting delays or shifting of schedules or resources can be handled effectively and efficiently both during the crisis and after it has been solved. The basic premise is that proactive rather than reactive management is the differentiating factor between organizations. The proactive management handles all situations and gets the job done. The reactive management is forever concentrating on the day-to-day problems and never progresses.

Non-project–group involvement

It is impossible to find a conversion project without some amount of contact or interface with people who are outside the conversion project team. Referring to the organizational diagram presented earlier in this chapter, this contact would be represented by the user liaisons and the user groups.

No matter what the company or organization, it is ultimately the user community that the computer systems were originally constructed for. It is key to the success of the conversion project that the user community be involved not only from the standpoint of dictating functional necessities but the actual acceptance testing as well. To achieve this, the user community must be aware of the progress of the conversion project and when the testing requirements will be satisfied and by how many resources. This is the responsibility of both the steering committee and the user liaisons. Ideally the steering committee will always have a representative from the user community whose responsibility is to communicate with the remainder of the user organizations. This is a tremendous burden on one or even two individuals when the overall organization is quite large. It is here that the user liaisons are more than just focal points of information for the project team. These liaisons also act as central communication points for the project team, keeping specific user groups abreast of the progress most pertinent to their situation.

Conversion Planning

The conversion of any software system from one machine or operating system to another requires the performance of many skills and jobs. It is essential to have a detailed plan that spells out the tasks that are to be performed, the generic skill required, and the time frame in which they are to be done. To do this accurately requires careful analysis and experience in the art of estimating. To accomplish any goal people must plan their work and work their plan. Figure 4.3 depicts the eight phases that must be blended harmoniously in the planning of a conversion.

Inventory analysis

One of the first things that must be established in a conversion is the amount of inventory that is to be converted and how this inventory relates to itself. To establish this inventory there are three phases; scanning, mapping, and reconciliation. Each of these topics is discussed separately in the following sections.

Figure 4.3 The eight phases of plan development.

Scanning. Although this subject was briefly discussed in Chapter 2, scanning has been included in this chapter in a summary fashion for the sake of completeness.

Scanning represents the method by which source code, JCL, data files, and other source files are examined. This may be accomplished in a variety of ways, but the most common is via automated means. This scanning software is generally parameter-driven and allows the user flexibility in defining what environment is being scanned.

Source files are scanned for items such as files used, number of database calls, number of subprograms called, frequency of specialized calls, and lines of overall code. This scanning facilitates not only the secondary step in inventory analysis—mapping—but allows for the proper formulation of estimating coefficients (discussed later in this chapter).

JCL scanning provides information on the number of job steps involved in any one job, the number and type of files required (including temporary, sequential, relational or database), and how programs are used in terms of sequence. This again facilitates the secondary phase of mapping.

Data files are scanned to determine the number of records and content integrity. Content integrity is important for two reasons: The first is to predict the amount of nonsense data present in the current system. It is important to know whether high values or low values have been used to fill in numerical data items when not entered directly by the system users. A second but somewhat obscure reason is to verify that the data layouts are the ones that are actually being used and to verify that the data present on each record matches the specified layout. It is this type of analysis that will later aid in complexity analysis and formulating estimating coefficients.

Other types of source files that are scanned are procedure files and copylib members. Procedures are scanned in the same manner as JCL files and for the same reasons. Copylib members are scanned to determine layouts and the number of different layouts certain files may have.

Scanning in total allows the conversion project team to more accurately determine what they are facing in terms of sheer numbers, as well as give them a solid basis upon which to develop the remainder of the analysis that is required in a project of this type.

Mapping. Mapping is the art of putting together the information gathered from the scanning process into a logical tabular format. An example of mapping is the cross-reference table between files and programs. A secondary chart would show the relationship between jobs and programs. These charts, often referred to as cross-reference tables, can be set up in many different ways and can serve many purposes. The main objective of mapping is to serve as a single source for establishing what data files, programs, or job streams are related to each other. This minimizes the risks when converting a file, program, or job stream because it provides a checklist for ensuring that nothing has been missed.

A second objective of the mapping exercise identifies the interrelationships of files and programs. This is important in conversions, since it is inevitable that there will be some change in the logic flow of programs. Without this road map it would be a much more difficult task to determine what other programs, files, or job streams have been affected by the simplest of changes.

Inventory reconciliation. Reconciliation of the inventory is the last step in inventory analysis. This is the examination of all source programs and data files to ensure that there is no duplication or omission. It also ensures that no old versions have crept into the list to be converted. Finally, the last check performed in this step is the elimination of programs no longer used or desired.

This reconciliation will accurately reflect the true numbers of source programs, files, and JCL that will be involved in the conversion. Without this accuracy, any plans or schedules that will be produced later will add little meaning to the true scope of the project. It is always better to spend more time at the beginning of a project to make sure of what you have to deal with than be surprised later on and then have to go back to management to explain the reason for the request for more time or more money or both.

Complexity analysis

The second most important analysis performed is known as complexity analysis. This examines the peculiarities of the source code and language and the translation alternatives that are afforded this project.

Source profile. Knowledge is power and power in a conversion comes from understanding exactly what one is dealing with. Scanning is able to provide numbers of calls to subprograms and the number of calls generally used within the programs. What scanning does not provide is the detailed understanding of how these calls are structured and what they require. This may range from parameters and their specific order to specific language constraints. This is more commonly known as performing a source profile.

It is important to document not only the normal circumstances of the source language (and possibly the source machine) but the idiosyncrasies as well. A good example of machine idiosyncrasies is the difference between ASCII machines and EBCDIC machines. Sort-collating sequences are different for ASCII and EBCDIC. Signed numeric packed on an ASCII-based machine might have its sign bit on the left side while the EBCDIC machine contains the sign bit on the right. Possibly only line-by-line or field-by-field data-entry screens are available on the source machine while the target machine offers a wide variety of different data-entry facilities. Each project has its unique problems presented to the project team. It is the job of the project manager and that of the project team, to discover the special quirks in the current environment and to document them in addition to the normal operations and specifics of the source language. This will afford the project team a single, documented solution when a problem arises during the actual conversion execution. Once a translation alternative has been selected for each circumstance, it should also be documented. The source profile allows the project team as a whole to make a more intelligent decision on translation alternatives or tradeoffs.

Translation alternatives. Translation alternatives are conscious choices made by the project manager or the project team in solving conversion problems. These conscious choices are made only after careful analysis of the inventory and the complexity of the conversion project and its components.

Translation alternatives may run the gamut between a fully automated software translator and a complete manual translation. Each decision must be detailed so that all members of the team understand why the decision was made. Alternatives are chosen for each part of the conversion and are not meant to be blanket decisions. For environments that are converting from many different source languages or machines there will be many necessary alternatives.

The key word in this discussion is *alternative*. There are no hard-and-fast rules. Choices available to the project team must be evaluated until one alternative is determined better than the rest. Remember also that the best alternative in one situation is not necessarily the best in another even if the situations are similar. Each alternative must be weighed against the particular circumstance in which it is to be applied.

Once the reasonable alternatives have been selected, they must be analyzed to determine what resources and effort will be required to implement them. The expectancy level of the alternative, once implemented, must also be analyzed. For example, assume that an alternative of an automated translator tool has been chosen. One must now know what special circumstances it provides for, if the project team must modify this tool, how long it will take, and what the percentage of translation will be.

This type of analysis will determine if the alternative is viable within the constraints of the project. Often a decision is made to use a specific alternative without doing a full analysis of what impact this solution will have on the conversion project. It is too late when it is learned that this was an incorrect choice.

Estimating and coefficients

Estimating has been called the exacting science of crystal-ball gazing. This is not altogether an untrue statement. Estimating is nothing more than the educated guess of a professional who has experienced the exact same phenomenon or something that approximates it. The most experienced professional can never be expected to be more exact than ±10 percent on an estimate, even assuming that every detail concerning the project has already been supplied. Under normal circumstances, the project manager will be expected to produce the conversion plan estimates. A potential problem here is that he/she probably does not have conversion experience and may not have any experience at all with the new target environment. In this case estimating becomes pure conjecture and guesswork. Unfortunately, the manager may be held responsible when the plan developed from these estimates does not even come close to reality. It must be pointed out that the utilization of outside resource personnel specializing in conversion activities will greatly reduce the risk associated with poor estimates, since more experience in this type of planning can be brought to bear upon the problem.

To alleviate the problem of poor estimating, enlist the aid of trusted people who have either experience in the type of conversion currently envisioned or at least experience in the new target environment. The estimates received should be realistic and neither pessimistic or optimistic. In addition, estimates for the translation alternatives must be weighed against this knowledge. It is always a sound idea to require at least three estimates. When dealing with a conversion, determine why there are vast differences in opinion if such major differences occur.

Coefficients and estimates have been previously mentioned. Coefficients are static estimates that will be used throughout the development of the conversion schedule. Examples of coefficients are: for every 100 lines of source code it will take three hours to translate, compile, and test the new code; every seven jobs under the current environment will become one job in the new environment; due to a learning curve factor, the first three programs translated will take 80 hours each while successive ones will average 60 hours each. These are but a few of the static estimates termed coefficients.

Another aspect of coefficients used in a conversion project concerns split responsibilities for any given task. For example, a decision may be made that involves a senior analyst's time as well as an analyst's time. The coefficient decided upon may be that for all source code translation, the split in time is 40 percent senior analyst and 60 percent analyst. These coefficients will have an effect on the type and amount of resources required when the overall conversion plan is formulated and costed.

Resource analysis

The awareness of the resources available and the resources required is essential in determining any conversion plan. In examining the resources available, examine not only the resources internal to the company but those that are available from external sources as well.

Internal resources.   One of the key factors in any project is the ability to capitalize on the organization's internal expertise. To ascertain the caliber of people, review the experience of all available personnel, their respective skill levels, and any of their proven or untried skills. Doing this investigation requires the aid of the people themselves. Resumés should be brought up to date to include any recent education or training. Interview each individual to determine factors that cannot be readily described on paper (such as enthusiasm, presence, etc.).

Once an overall evaluation of each individual has been made, the task of matching the appropriate resource to the requirements of the conversion project may begin. This is by no means a simple task and should not be taken lightly. Many factors must be weighed and care taken in deciding on resource assignment. One of the critical decision factors is knowing when there is no suitable single person or combination of resource personnel for the requirement. The second scenario is slightly easier to deal with since many resources can be applied to a single requirement. The first scenario is the more difficult of the two and leads into the second topic, external resource analysis.

External resources.   There comes a point when one cannot match resources to a conversion project's requirements because the necessary skill or skills are not available within the confines of the organization. At this time it will become necessary to examine what skills are available from external sources. There are many types of organizations available that can fulfill certain specific requirements. The preference is to deal with one organization that can supply all the requirements. This will avoid multiple points of contact and the usual communication and finger-pointing problems that arise in a multivendor project. This is not to say that a hardware vendor will not be able to get along with a consulting firm even when their motives may be different. However, multiple firms with the same competing motivation tend to have negative effects upon a project.

When analyzing an external resource, check for certain crucial factors, including:

- Has this company done this type of work before?
- Are the proposed people familiar with this type of work and have they worked specifically on a project of this nature?
- What are the specific backgrounds of the proposed people?
- Does the company foster and maintain a conversion methodology?

These are important questions and criteria when choosing an external resource. You must weigh all these factors before proposing your choice to the steering committee for approval, as external resources will add a definite cost to the project.

Schedule development

When all the analysis has been performed on both the technical and the nontechnical aspects of the conversion, it is time to develop a detailed execution schedule.

To develop the schedule, gather all the information from the analysis phases and put them in some logical progression. An example of this is baking a cake. You cannot bake the ingredients before mixing them and then hope to have a cake; you mix all the ingredients and then bake them. To aid in this development there are many mainframe tools, such as PROJACS from IBM, and many PC-based products such as Project Manager Workbench from Applied Business Technology, and Microsoft's MSPROJECT. Generally these are PERT/CPM-oriented products that allow a certain amount of flexibility in defining and outlining a project. In choosing which manner to do the detail scheduling, be it manual or automated, find out what other information is desired from the ongoing tracking and monitoring of the schedule when complete. Only personal preference or company standards will ultimately decide which of the forms the schedule is developed in.

In general, any schedule may be broken down into three distinct components: phases, activities, and tasks. Each of these components represents a successive breakdown of the composition of the project. A phase such as target environment preparation, may be considered an overall goal. A phase in itself is a major milestone and therefore should be comprised of other milestones. These are the activities. Both phases and activities should consist of start and end dates. In turn, activities are broken down into the tasks that go into achieving the milestone. It is how these tasks are defined that is the major challenge in developing a reasonable and realistic schedule.

The definition of each task in terms of effort must be carefully done. Each task must be not only a discrete portion of effort but constrained in a time frame that makes measurement a reasonable factor. For example, a single task should rarely span more than a two-week time frame. This allows a better understanding of how a task is progressing and at the same time whether or not the estimates for the task have been correct. The key point here is the ability to predict overruns or underruns so that the schedule may be readjusted.

Another important aspect in defining tasks within a schedule is to avoid preassigning specific resource personnel to a task. All task-development and time-frame estimates must be determined in a generic sense without considering specific personnel skills or assignments. The results from the resource analysis will determine which resource is matched to which task but only after the schedule is completed.

The final duty that must be performed when developing the schedule for a conversion is establishing the dependencies among the different tasks. The dependencies may be among tasks within the same activity or among tasks in different activities or phases. This allows for critical path determination. The critical path for a project determines the key tasks and how slippage on any one of these tasks affects the tasks that are dependent on it. It is the main tool for determining if the project will be completed in a timely fashion or not.

Once all of the above details have been taken care of, an initial project schedule is created. The information imbedded in this schedule will determine, or at least aid in determining, the numbers of resource types required to perform the conversion project and at what point in time they must be activated. At this point one can apply the actual resources gleaned from the resource analysis against the tasks. In its finished state, the schedule becomes an important tool for the conversion project but not a static thing. The schedule must be updated constantly and consistently with actual information as work progresses, and must be readjusted with refined estimates as newer and more accurate information becomes available. In short, the project schedule should become the most important tool used to ascertain the current status of the team and how many people and how long it will take to move to the next point.

Project costing

Within any project there are certain costs. These costs may be either fixed or variable. Fixed costs are generally one-time costs such as the cost for a software tool, a new terminal, or a desk. Variable costs are costs that change over time or costs that are calculated based on a factor and multiplied by the quantity associated with the factor. A good example of variable cost is the electricity used in homes. As more electricity is used the monthly cost becomes higher. The same rules apply within a conversion project. There will be certain fixed costs over the life of the project and certain variable ones.

The most important cost factor in a conversion project is labor. This is one of the largest variable costs associated with the project. A common belief is that the cost of the conversion is small because employees are doing the project and their salaries have to be paid no matter what. This is a misconception. Regardless of who is paying the salaries there is an associated cost to the project. Each hour spent or estimated to be spent should be multiplied by the hourly rate of the employee plus the percentage of salary that goes into making up fringe benefits such as health care.

Additional costs to consider are rental charges for equipment, space, and the cost of computer time if time has to spent on a time-sharing system, and many other incidentals. In general most people only consider the cost of external resources as a project cost. This could not be further from the truth. Only when all costs, both internal and external, fixed and variable, are taken into account can true cost justification be done.

As discussed previously in the section on scheduling, it is important to determine the approximate cost of the project in total as well as the cost for each phase. This will allow not only senior management to understand when and how the money is going to be spent, it also allows the project manager to monitor expenditures against tasks and milestones. This provides the ability to switch more expensive resource personnel away from tasks that could be handled by less costly personnel and put them on other critical items where their talent and cost are more appropriate.

It is important to remember that the project manager is not only responsible for completing the conversion but also has a fiscal responsibility to the organization to ensure that the monies are spent judiciously.

Phase life cycle identification

Just as a development project has a predefined life cycle, a conversion project also has a life cycle all its own. Everything has a beginning, a middle, and an end. Within a conversion project, these are the start-up, the execution, and the implementation. Each of these phases in turn can be broken into their respective components.

Within the start-up phase of a conversion there is the orientation, the source-environment preparation, the analysis, and the planning phases. The execution phase sees the inventory preparation, target-environment preparation, translation, documentation, and maintenance changes. The last phase, implementation, has parallel testing and production turnover.

Each one of these subphases is a major milestone within a conversion project and the components are activities. No matter how one breaks up the components of a conversion during the planning phase, the major activities mentioned above should always be included.

Within the start-up phase orientation, analysis, and planning have already been discussed. What has not been discussed until now is the source-environment preparation. This activity includes not only knowing and isolating the software that is to be converted, but planning and preparing for an environment for the conversion project team. This can include additional space, more terminals, and additional administrative assistance. In addition, this activity includes preparing the remainder of the organization for the conversion in terms of awareness and possible commitment.

Within the execution phase inventory preparation is the logical bundling of the software that is to be converted. This logical bundling must be done in a manner that makes sense from both a functional point of view and a physical one. The bundles must be functionally connected and at the same time manageable. Avoid converting a complete system composed of 1000 programs in a single chunk. The next activity within this phase is target-environment preparation. This is comprised of installing the new target environment, setting up the user I.D.'s, putting in the appropriate security levels, and installing any system-management tools and DASD tools. This activity sometimes includes the construction associated with a new machine environment, but this is dependent on the type of conversion and target-machine environment. The next execution activity is translation. This is the actual conversion of the bundled software. The conversion itself may be made through either automated or manual means or a combination of both. The next two activities, documentation and maintenance changes, can be considered parallel activities within the execution phase. Documentation is the noting of any changes caused by the conversion to the existing documentation or runbooks, while maintenance changes include making any changes or additions to the software, per user requests, that were precluded from the original software because of the conversion activity. It should be noted that within each of the activities of translation and maintenance changes, extensive testing is included.

The final phase, implementation, contains the activities of parallel testing (when possible) and production turnover. Parallel testing is where the newly converted system is monitored against the old system to ensure complete integrity before the new system is officially put into production and the old system is turned off. The last activity in this phase and in the conversion life cycle is production turnover. This activity includes the formal implementation of the converted software and includes educating the production staff (if necessary) to run or monitor the new software environment.

Although this is a rather concise description of the life cycle of a conversion, it demonstrates that there are many things involved in a conversion. No matter how insignificant or self-evident a task or an activity is, it should always be accounted for somewhere in the life cycle.

Project start-up plan

Before beginning a conversion, plan what will be needed to start the project off on the right foot. This should include space, terminals, and what type of organization (from management's perspective) needs to be put into place and who should be resident within this organization. This will become, in effect, a high-level project plan with a detailed initial phase.

The key to a conversion project is the ability and dedication of all persons involved in planning a course of action and then following that plan. Keep in mind that plans are never etched in granite but are there to guide and help evaluate. Murphy's law will always come into play in the best of situations. If you believe in the saying "the best laid plans of mice and men so oft agone a-gley," then anticipate and replan.

Productivity in a Dynamic Environment

The most important reasons for any conversion are the benefits that the whole organization will gain when the conversion is completed. One of the major tasks confronting the organization, however, is surviving the conversion period. An organization must be able to stay productive throughout the entire process. To do this you must understand the obstacles and take the appropriate measures.

Recognizing disruptions

For those familiar with renovating a house or redecorating a bathroom, the sheer mention of these activities brings horror stories to the mind. Yet these same people seem to have made it through the experience relatively unscathed. The reason is quite simple. These people recognized the disruptions that were going to occur and planned around them so that their normal daily life was disturbed to a minimum. The same must hold true for a conversion. The organization must recognize the two different types of disruptions that will occur and make decisions on how to minimize the effect these disruptions will have.

Physical disruptions

The major disruption in a conversion is the physical disruption caused by a variety of activities. These can include the construction of a new computer facility, the additional space required to support a larger staff, the temporary space required to accommodate external consultants during the conversion, and a host of other smaller yet equally disruptive items. If one is aware at the onset of the project of the types of physical disruptions that will occur, then an offsetting course of action may be planned. In the case of additional space being required, trailers may be rented and placed in close proximity so that access to required resources is simplified. If being in close contact is not a high priority, additional office space may be rented or unused space may be converted. This is just an oversimplified version, but it does demonstrate that for every problem there can be a reasonable solution. Whether these problems have a negative effect on the organization or not depends largely on the effort spent at the beginning of the conversion process to identify and overcome these obstacles through careful planning.

Logical disruptions

A logical disruption occurs when the normal flow of work within an organization is disturbed. A good example of this is when users are informed that the turnaround time for modification requests has now been expanded from two days to possibly two years. This, of course, will not win popularity awards within the user community. Other, more insidious forms of logical disruptions are the hours that will have to be spent by users and managers in confirming test results and in discussing the functionality of the systems being converted. These necessary hours will take time away from the normal routines followed in the user departments.

These types of disruptions are not as simple as physical ones, as they are not as concrete in terms of actual resources required. Although it should be realized at the beginning of the project that testing is mandatory, the exact number of hours required and precisely who will conduct the testing is usually a gray area. These items are more accurately forecasted as the need arises. The problem the organization faces is to be prepared for these disturbances before they happen and have a plan to minimize their effect. Due to the nature of this type of disturbance, careful planning must be done. This plan should include education of the departments that will have disruptions placed upon them so that they comprehend what will be demanded of them when the time comes. During the execution phase of the conversion, sufficient time must be allowed for the person or persons affected to reallocate their time. This is necessary so that they can not only do the job that is normally required of them but include this new responsibility as well.

It has been said that there are no such things as problems, there exist only opportunities. In terms of a conversion, it is the project manager's duty as well as that of the steering committee to weigh the opportunity costs that will present themselves based upon the disruptions that will inevitably occur.

Managing for business as usual

Throughout the entire conversion life cycle it is extremely important for the organization to be cognizant of the impacts and benefits derived as work progresses. The critical factor is management's commitment to improving the current position through the conversion and, at the same time, to not be led into believing that the conversion is a panacea for all of its ills. Management must be made aware of the added strain that will be put upon the organization throughout the course of the conversion. They must be mindful that progress has a price and, within a conversion, this price is the disruption of normal activities. Counteracting these disruptions will require painstaking planning and the ability to weigh alternatives and make clear and timely decisions. The critical importance of maintaining the business must supercede all other considerations, even if the impact is upon the conversion.

It is the challenge of management to keep the status quo within the organization. A conversion should be thought of as managing two separate business entities within the same organization. The data processing department is attempting to change itself while at the same time servicing the entire organization. The user community is straining under the pressures put on it to assist in the conversion while demanding the same level of service it has grown accustomed to.

The challenge of managing for business as usual must be considered top priority and made the responsibility of not only top management but everyone within the organization. It is essential that everyone be cognizant of the trauma that the organization will have to endure during the conversion process, and that every effort must be made to ensure that the company survives. It is one thing to have a business problem solved by a conversion, it is another to have the organization harmed by the very same thing that is supposed to help.

5

Preparing for the New Environment

Embracing the New Technology

Recognizing the magnitude of a conversion

The intent of this entire section, "Preparing for the New Environment," is to demonstrate the need for planning at all levels of a conversion. All too often companies enter into a major conversion project focused entirely on the translation of application systems. Converting to a large systems environment involves much more than that. Problems that typically arise during a conversion can usually be attributed to inadequate planning; but, more often than not, these problems center on something other than the translation process. A number of organizations have successfully completed their conversion only to be disappointed with the results. The objectives they established at the onset of the project were not entirely met. To truly gain the benefits of the new environment, the data center may need to change the way it does business. This means that procedures, methods, schedules, techniques, functions, and people must adapt to the new environment and not the other way around. When charged with the responsibility of a conversion, the ability to envision this concept cannot be overemphasized. Plan for it and act on it accordingly to truly complete a successful conversion project.

The preceding chapter may have painted a gloomy picture of what's involved in the conversion process. The intent was to inform you, when faced with a major conversion project, of the real scope of this project as well as the effort required to successfully complete the project.

Undoubtedly you have heard the war stories and horror stories of other DP shops which have gone through a major conversion and are recovering from a major conversion or are still attempting to complete their conversion. Unfortunately, all those stories that you've heard are probably true. It really doesn't have to be that way, though. Many organizations have not only survived the conversion but have significantly benefited from the process—although they generally wouldn't want to go through it again. You should be able to successfully complete a conversion with minimal loss of sleep and without worry of an unplanned career adjustment. The remainder of this section is dedicated to providing you with some practical information and useful tips for making it all work.

Recognizing the Scope of the Project

There are four critically important concepts which must be recognized, understood, and accepted to ensure success in the conversion process. First, there is a lot more to this project than installing new hardware, loading a new operating system, and converting programs. When changing hardware vendors, operating systems, or architectures, establishing the new operating environment is at least as important as the application conversion itself.

Conversion is really a global term and the typical conversion project involves many different issues of concern. Figure 5.1. illustrates a big picture view of the typical conversion project. It can be seen from this illustration that in addition to the application systems, the project must address technical issues such as network, hardware, operating system, etc. These technical issues are usually expected in advance and are usually well planned and staffed. There are a number of procedural and management issues which also must be examined, planned, created, or modified. The tasks include security, system management, education and training, standards and procedures, disaster recovery, and organization and staffing. These are the issues which tend to get little attention or are not addressed at all.

Many organizations that get into trouble during the conversion process tend to overlook many issues or do not recognize the importance or magnitude of effort required to establish and support a totally new environment. The focus of their attention is the application systems. It's easy to understand their view of this process, for

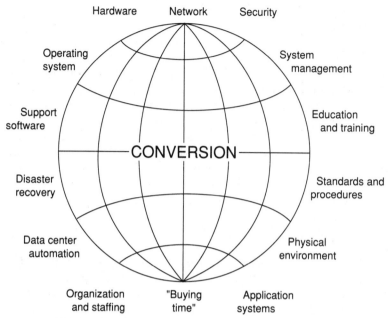

Hardware   Network   Security

Operating system   System management

Support software   Education and training

CONVERSION

Disaster recovery   Standards and procedures

Data center automation   Physical environment

Organization and staffing   "Buying time"   Application systems

Figure 5.1 The big picture.

their applications are what this whole computer system and conversion is about. Conversions are performed for a number of reasons: to provide the availability of new and better applications, to provide greater system capacity (for the applications), to provide greater throughput or quicker response time (for the applications), as well as a number of other application-related issues. Users and corporate management are not concerned with what the equipment looks like, how it works, or even how state-of-the-art it may be. Operating systems, programming languages, DASD, and other things described by other DP buzzwords are of no concern to them. Their concerns are the capability, availability, and responsiveness of the system to their application needs and desires. The environment necessary to support these applications must be present at all times, without limitations or restrictions. Making it all work is just "something the folks in data processing do."

Conversion—a corporatewide project

The second important concept is recognizing the conversion as a corporate project. The decision to convert is a business decision, as presented in Chapter 1, and not a data-processing decision. In order to succeed the conversion project must have the commitment and involvement of MIS, the user community and corporate management. (See Figure 5.2.)

Corporate management must act as the sponsors of this major project. An affinitive bond must be established between corporate management and MIS during the course of this project. Gaining the sponsorship of corporate management can be a task in itself. In most organizations, data processing is viewed as a necessary expense. Simply justifying the need for a conversion is usually not good enough. It will require a good deal of salesmanship. This will be a significant project carrying a fairly hefty price tag. It is highly unlikely that corporate management will accept sponsorship unless they are totally convinced of its need and completely confident in the enterprise's ability to successfully pull it off.

Communications—avoiding the vacuum

The third important concept in a successful conversion project is keeping open lines of communication. This project, a corporate-wide effort, will affect the entire enterprise. It will require significant funding, extended for what may seem like an eternity, and leave a lot of disruption in its wake. The old saying, "no news is good news," certainly doesn't apply to conversion projects. Keeping the conversion project in a vacuum can generate a multitude of problems, most of them completely unwarranted. The broad scope of this project will naturally generate interest and concern from all areas within the

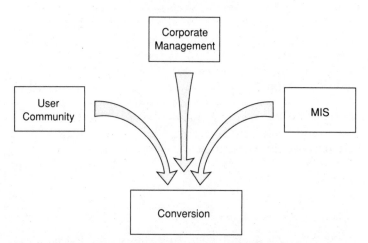

Figure 5.2 Conversion is not simply a DP or MIS project. It requires the support, commitment, and involvement of corporate management and the user community.

company. Users will want to know how the conversion will effect them. Management, both corporate and departmental, will be concerned with schedules and budgets. Other projects, delayed because of the conversion, will be another constant source of pressure. It is essential that effective and timely communications be provided to all interested parties. Figure 5.3. illustrates four key components for effective communication during a conversion:

- Setting expectations for the new environment
- Establishing a public relations program
- Maintaining open lines of communication
- Managing visibility

Setting expectations

The new environment is being prepared to provide new and better information-processing capabilities for the enterprise. What these new and better capabilities are must be communicated to the users. If not, their support will be difficult if not impossible to obtain. If the users' expectations are not properly set at the onset of the project, they will manufacture their own. These expectations may prove difficult to meet.

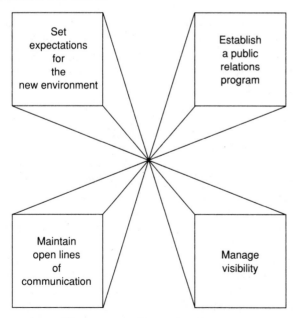

Figure 5.3 Elements of effective communication are essential during conversion.

A major international corporation, headquartered in the Chicago area, was driven to a conversion in order to achieve added capacity for their existing information systems. These existing applications were generally adequate for their business needs, but the organization was expanding rapidly and found it very difficult to add additional terminals as new divisions were acquired or established. To meet the needs generated by their growth, they ventured into a major project which involved an upgrade of equipment and a new, more sophisticated operating system. The actual project was billed as an upgrade of computing resources and assigned as an MIS project. Because of this upgrade status, the user community was not expected to be directly affected by the project and was not only excluded from the planning process, but was not provided with any information beyond the fact that it was happening and was necessary.

During the yearlong effort required to establish the new environment and migrate all application systems, the user community developed their own expectations of just what this upgrade would do for them. Different user groups developed slightly different expectations, but in general they expected to see better response time and significant application enhancements.

At the completion of the project additional capacity was achieved as planned. The users, however, were not at all pleased with the results. The new processor, although much larger than the previous computer, did not provide their expected response-time improvements. In fact, because of the additional resource consumption of the more sophisticated operating system, no visible performance benefits were realized by the users. The users were also disappointed to find that their applications still retained their old restrictions and limitations, with no signs of enhancement. After putting up with numerous disruptions over the past year with no real payback at the end, they were not very understanding when told they had never been promised any enhancements. Needless to say the user community complained to corporate management, citing the project's failure to meet their expectations. MIS, unfortunately, became the scapegoat of the situation. Instead of being applauded for successfully achieving their goals, corporate management presented them with another project to correct their mistakes.

This example was presented to show just how these situations can get out of hand when unrealistic or uncontrolled expectations are allowed to develop. Perhaps if the project goals were clearly identified and discussed with management and the user community before actual project initiation, the scope of the project might have been changed to incorporate some of the user community's desires. Even without considering a change of scope, proper communication of the project's objectives and limitations could have set real expectations in the user's minds rather than leaving them to their imaginations.

Establish public relations

A successful technique for establishing the right expectations is through a public relations campaign prior to initiating the project. This may seem rather frivolous; however, it can be quite effective and doesn't really require a significant amount of effort or expense to accomplish. Most organizations have some established house organ which can be utilized to promote the conversion project. If not, a simple MIS newsletter can be prepared as a convenient and informal vehicle for communicating current plans and activities to the user community. Announcing conversion project plans in this manner provides an opportunity to properly define the project's goals and objectives in nonspecialist's terms rather than technical jargon, and communicate those ideas to the entire organization. This same vehicle can then be used to communicate progress as well as other events which may affect the users.

MIS personnel should not be overlooked in the PR campaign. In large shops where all MIS personnel are not necessarily privy to department plans and projects, effective communication during the project will be essential to staff morale. Rumors spread rapidly and can do serious damage if not quickly quashed. With the changing environment personnel will become very concerned with their future in the organization and how the conversion will affect them directly. Most people within MIS will react positively to news of a conversion, generally viewing it as a new challenge and an opportunity for personal growth. A lack of communication or information, however, may cause needless concern, raising suspicions that something's wrong or that management is hiding something from them.

It's also a good idea to announce the conversion project to MIS staff members before publicly announcing it to the rest of the company. Providing the staff with advance knowledge of corporate plans, even if that knowledge is provided immediately before public announcement, can produce an immediate psychological boost to MIS staff morale and build a sense of team spirit within the MIS organization.

Maintain open communications

Regularly scheduled progress reporting is an absolute requirement during the conversion project. Progress reports are intended to maintain open lines of communication by:

Informing management about current status, progress, problems, and decisions

Documenting various events during the project

Helping to monitor and control the project

Although progress reports are generally directed to management and the steering committee, general project progress should be communicated to the entire enterprise. This public progress-reporting should contain a summary of the key events which have occurred and those which are scheduled to occur in the near future, highlighting issues which may be of particular interest to the user community. These reports should be provided regularly, although not necessarily with the same frequency as management reports. Usually monthly reporting is sufficient; more frequent reporting may be overambitious. Whatever means are used for the PR campaign (MIS newsletter, house organ, etc.), they are also the best method for communicating the project's status.

Manage visibility

The last important area of communication which should be addressed is managing visibility. Managing visibility can almost be considered an art form, although it really is nothing more than good data-center management practice. Managing visibility is defined as controlling the enterprise's view of MIS. Negative visibility should be reduced and positive visibility promoted. This does not mean that MIS should hide problems. The best method for eliminating negative visibility is eliminating problems. This may seem like an impossible task, but most problems that affect users can be eliminated or at least greatly reduced with proper management controls.

Although a good PR program will help the relationship between the user community and MIS, actions do indeed speak louder than words. MIS will continue to be judged based on their results and not their intentions. During the conversion project, when the new environment is under construction and the staff is trying to learn their jobs, quite a bit can go wrong and probably will. How the department handles these potential problems and their prevention is a major part of this management of visibility.

Establishing good, solid procedures and controls in the existing environment as well as the new environment will greatly aid in the management of visibility. Three particular areas of concentration will provide the best results:

Enforcing system management concepts

Implementing adequate security methods and procedures

Establishing a "help desk"

System management is the process of tightly controlling the production environment. Its purpose is simply to provide a controlled, stable environment for production work within MIS. System management concepts generally consists of change management, problem management, configuration or inventory management, and quality assurance.

Change management is a system management method designed to protect the production environment by controlling change. It is not intended to inhibit change but rather to ensure that the production environment will remain stable and able to function as changes are introduced into the environment. Change management should apply to any change or activity which may in some way affect the production environment. Programs, batch job-control, network modifications, software updates, and any work done within the physical environment such as electrical work in the computer room, are but a few of the types of changes which must be controlled by change management.

Change management should not be confused with the typical work requests most shops use to document requests for modifications to application systems. The user is never directly involved in the change management process. Change management is strictly a procedure internal to MIS.

Using an application modification as an example, the change management process begins after the work has actually been performed and it is ready for implementation. The modification is made to the appropriate programs, tested to the satisfaction of management and the requester, and the necessary turnover documentation is prepared. When the complete package has been reviewed as described in the documented production turnover procedure, the originator (the programmer in this case, not the user who requested the modification) prepares a change request form and submits it to the change coordinator. Change management coordination is basically a clerical function. The coordinator accepts the change request, ensures that it is correctly completed, logs the change request, and distributes copies to the members of the change committee. The change coordinator also monitors the progress of change requests throughout the process, reporting the results of the changes implemented (successful, unsuccessful, outstanding, scheduled, etc.) to the change committee.

The change committee is composed of MIS management. Change

committee meetings should be regularly scheduled, usually once each week, for less than an hour in duration. The change committee reviews changes submitted, grants approval for the changes, and schedules their implementation. The committee meetings are not intended to serve as a forum for explaining the nature of the actual work performed. Committee members should already be acquainted with the scope of the work performed and its purpose prior to this meeting.

Generally, change committees only review those changes which could be considered high-risk and those which may severely impact processing if their implementation failed. Routine changes and low-impact changes are not usually reviewed by the committee, but must still follow the defined procedure. With each change submitted, a backout procedure must be documented. This procedure is designed to be used if something goes wrong during implementation.

Problem management is the formal logging and tracking of reported problems. The purpose of this process is to ensure that problems are resolved in a reasonable time frame. The problem management coordinator (again a clerical function) maintains the problem log and reports problem resolution status to management. The problem management coordinator should also perform a periodic analysis of problem history to determine trends and identify reoccurring problems.

Some technique to flag problems which have remained unresolved beyond a designated period of time should be developed and implemented. Problem priority levels should be defined along with time limits for resolving those problems. Problems that are not resolved and closed within the allotted time should be brought to the attention of management. The problem management system should also provide a direct interface to the change management system. In a stable environment, most problems are the result of change, or else change will be initiated to resolve reported problems. In either case, there is a direct relationship between change and problem management.

The problem management process should be used by anyone who has a need to report a problem. The problems logged and tracked by this process are not restricted to the production environment and should be used for the entire organization.

Configuration management is actually a simple inventory-control process. Most MIS organizations use configuration management to keep track of all equipment and vendor-supplied software, although it can be used for other purposes. A typical configuration management system would provide a means of documenting each component designated for control by the system. This documentation would include specific items of information such as component description, serial number, date of purchase or lease, physical location, vendor data, maintenance contract information, etc. Many shops also use this system to record equipment failure history. Its value in alerting MIS management of lease or maintenance contract renewal dates can prove to be an effective cost tool. Many vendors will automatically renew leases and maintenance contracts unless cancellation is requested in writing in advance of their expiration. The database of information provided by configuration management, can also serve as a tool for verifying vendor invoices.

Quality assurance is basically the administration and enforcement of set procedures and standards within the MIS organization. Although quality assurance is the responsibility of everyone in MIS, the absolute responsibility rests upon the MIS manager. Most medium- and large-scale organizations will appoint a full-time quality assurance administrator to serve as the watchdog of the department. The quality assurance administrator serves as the enforcer of shop standards and administrator of all other system management procedures. The quality assurance administrator also is responsible for monitoring and controlling the production turnover process. Production turnover procedures generally describe the process, documentation, and other requirements essential to the orderly implementation of new or modified applications in the production environment.

Good security practices, particularly during the conversion project, can reduce unscheduled outages. Most damage caused by breaches of security in MIS are not the result of hackers, vandals, terrorists, or acts of God, but are usually caused by innocent mistakes made by MIS staff members. In a new environment, the typical MIS staff member is presented with a number of new toys. These people will be tempted by natural curiosity to investigate these new features to see just what they can do. In addition, because the staff is relatively new to the environment, they will be prone to making more mistakes than experienced people.

Although most security problems are the result of human error, the possibility of willful destruction must also be considered.

Physical security is the easiest form to implement. Data center accessibility can be restricted by mechanical or electronic locks. In most shops only operations personnel have the need to enter the computer room. Application personnel in the computer room running tests themselves or seeking test results, listings, or anything else, pose a needless security risk to the organization and disruption to operations.

Media protection and control is also essential to proper security.

Files that mysteriously disappear cause increased workloads and scheduling problems due to file re-creation runs. Testing with production data should be eliminated completely or at least severely restricted. Magnetic tape should never be allowed to leave the computer room or tape vault without specific authorization. Listings containing sensitive corporate data should not be discarded without first shredding.

Good security, preferably a good security package, will greatly reduce the potential of these problems. Password protection is the most common form of computer access control. A number of vendor-application packages provide at least this level of security. System security packages supply access control beyond password protection as well as more sophisticated means of protection for the environment. These packages will not only limit access to authorized users, but allow the definition of specific levels of access. User access can be easily limited to update or read operations. The ability to delete files can be entirely removed from their control.

Proper attention must be given to security design. Security packages are simply tools which can be used to implement desired levels of security within the system. Certain conditions which may exist in the current environment may require added levels of protection. For example, dial-up remote access and attached PC's can present additional security risks to the enterprise. Even with the use of sophisticated security software packages, once data is physically removed or copied from the base system it is no longer under the control of the security package. Authorization to read data also implies authority to copy data. If you can read a file, you can copy it; and the copy will not necessarily be protected by the security system.

The best possible time to implement a system security package is as soon as the environment has been established and before anyone is actively allowed to use the system. This is the condition that exists during a conversion project immediately before application development or conversion team personnel are introduced into the system environment. Implementing a security package after the system is operating as a production environment will be much more difficult and can present excessive risks to the production environment. The definition of security parameters or rules is a delicate process. Improperly defining security rules can virtually lock out system users and deny them access to their own application systems.

The purpose of the help desk is to provide a central point of contact for all system user problems and questions. A good, well functioning help desk, should be able to internally handle at least 80 percent of the typical problems reported to MIS. This is normally achievable because most problems called in by users tend to be procedural, repetitious, or really "nonproblem" problems. A nonproblem problem is one that requires no solution. This can mean that the problem was already discovered and corrected or a scheduling or procedural error occurred which can't be corrected but only prevented in the future. It can also mean that the user simply needed information or guidance. Many of these problem reports are easily addressed by the help desk administrator while on the phone with the user. Even though no real solution may have been offered by the help desk, most users are generally satisfied by the response they receive.

Those problems that do require some type of specialized attention can usually be easily identified and directed to the appropriate support personnel. The help desk administrator remains actively involved in the problem-resolution process, tracking resolution status, and providing updated information to the user and MIS management. One of the most important responsibilities of the help desk is keeping users informed of the status of their open problems and alerting them of scheduled events which may affect their service.

The help desk need not be staffed with technical personnel, although a number of organizations choose to do so. The help desk, besides providing a practical and important service to the enterprise, is actually an extension of the MIS/PR program. The ideal help desk administrator should possess strong interpersonal skills as well as excellent communication skills. The ideal candidate should also be able to grasp technical concepts at a general level as well as understand data-processing buzzwords in order to translate for the users. After a relatively short period of time, help desk personnel will experience the majority of the environment's most common problems and develop a practical semitechnical skill set in the process.

These three communication-related areas: setting expectations, progress reporting, and managing visibility can make your job considerably easier and allow more time to direct your attention to the real issues of conversion.

Opportunity vs. problem

The fourth and last important concept which must be understood and accepted is that this conversion is really an opportunity and not a problem. The conversion project presents an opportunity that data-processing shops rarely ever get: the opportunity to start over again. This doesn't mean that everything should be scrapped and redeveloped. This conversion will, however, present the opportunity to take a good, hard look at just how the shop functions. This is an excellent opportunity to clean up the shop and correct problems and inadequacies that may have plagued the MIS organization for years.

This cleanup operation will require that you remain open-minded. To be successful, it will require the reexamination of the accepted. Every aspect of the operation, procedures, methods, common practices, job descriptions, and standards are fair game in this reexamination. There should be no sacred cows.

Although this reexamination may at first appear to be a monumental task, it really isn't that difficult, and can normally be accomplished in a few weeks. Most of the areas that could use some sort of reworking are probably already known. The real work is the effort required to correct the deficiencies uncovered in the investigation. No matter how well organized or proficient the shop may be there are probably a number of areas that could be improved. You will more than likely be forced to revise your wish list and develop some type of ranking by priority or severity.

When examining the operation of the shop each area examined should be viewed as it would function in the new environment. Wherever possible the capabilities of the new environment should be applied. Many manual tasks or cumbersome procedures and methods may be totally unnecessary or at least greatly simplified. When finished with the evaluation, those areas selected for reworking should be included in project plans along with all other necessary conversion activities.

It is important to remember not to get too carried away during the evaluation process. Everything in the shop is not necessarily bad. Many of the methods developed over the years may work very well in the new environment. In fact, it may be quite difficult to come up with better ways of performing these activities. Gaining slight improvements in processes that already function well may not be worth the effort. Change for the sake of change should not become a hidden objective of this project. Change only what needs to be changed!

Restructuring the DP Organization

Information services vs. data processing

This book has used the terms *Management information services* and *data processing* somewhat interchangeably. In most usages, the correct term is actually management information services, or its common acronym, MIS. The term data processing (DP) has become somewhat archaic, still used by many organizations because of tradition rather than an accurate designation of the area's function. Today's management information services facility has really come a long way from the original data processing concept common in the 60s and early 70s. At that time the focus of the industry was mainly concentrated on the automation of standard business functions such as accounting, payroll, accounts receivable, etc. Today the automation of these functions is still supported; however, the primary mission of MIS is to supply management information and services vital to the success of the enterprise.

In the data-processing days, most systems were batch-oriented applications. These systems were scheduled and run periodically by the data center. Output was basically in the form of listings generated as an end result of running the applications. Information available to the users reflected the results of yesterday's processing or last month's activity.

Today the prevalent applications within MIS are on-line or real-time. New generations of applications have been developed to use computing for purposes that were only dreams 20 years ago. Last month's, last week's, or yesterday's information is no longer sufficient to remain competitive in the marketplace of the 90's and beyond. Users expect and demand instantaneous access to current and accurate information.

In the data-processing era, the DP department told the users what they would get in terms of functionality. The computer possessed a certain type of mystique, foreign to all but a select handful of technicians. Today the computer is commonplace, used for a number of everyday functions, and usually found in every home in one form or another. Users are more computer-literate, and make demands that MIS applications really fit their needs and desires. Terms such as "user-friendly," "interactive," etc., have cropped up along the way indicating the trend toward user responsiveness. Data processing has been forced to evolve into the user-oriented services organization that is today's management information services organization.

A successful MIS organization is now measured by the satisfaction of its users and the satisfaction of corporate management. In essence a successful MIS organization is a service-oriented organization. User satisfaction is gained by delivering quality services in a timely fashion. Corporate management, users themselves of information services, are also interested in the same quality of service but within the restrictions of a reasonable operating budget. Desired service levels and operating budget can become opposing forces if not properly and formally defined and controlled. If left solely to the expectations of users and typical management emphasis on cost reduction, MIS would be faced with service-level expectations which may be nearly impossible to meet. A proper balance of service vs. operating cost is key to a successful MIS organization.

To determine proper organization and staffing level requirements for the new environment, *service level objectives* should first be established. Service level objectives are predefined levels of expectation based on certain criteria or standards. Development of service level objectives must be prepared jointly between MIS and its users and should be approved by corporate management. These objectives must define the levels of availability and performance users can reasonably expect from the MIS organization. Because these objectives are jointly developed by MIS and the users, expectations should be reasonable and achievable. MIS management must then determine the operational costs associated with providing this agreed-upon service level and gain corporate management approval.

Specialization

The key to success in supporting a new, large systems environment during and after a conversion is *specialization.* In most environments that have evolved over the years many functions are typically performed by a variety of staff. No matter how large the organization is, however, certain key people are usually the backbone of the department. These key people are typically jacks-of-all-trades. They are the experts in everything and are usually called upon in a crisis to bail out the shop. They are always loyal and highly regarded within the department. They may serve as role models for the rest of the staff and their expertise is usually the product of many years of experience.

Unfortunately, when the environment is significantly changed, such as in a conversion, their expertise in the new environment is usually no greater than the rest of the staff. This is no reflection on their capabilities or potential but merely a product of what actually happens when the environment changes so dramatically.

This situation can have a profound effect on the operation of the data center. During the conversion process, and for some time thereafter, the organization can no longer be as dependent as it was on the skills and expertise of these people. Some other means of survival must be found.

Developing new expertise is the answer to this problem. New expertise, sufficient to support the new environment, can be developed through specialization. This specialization must be enforced by management by limiting personnel involvement in different aspects of the new environment. People must be strongly encouraged to restrict their involvement to their assigned areas of responsibility and concentrate their efforts on learning their new role in the organization. This will require a great deal of personal discipline for those staff members normally accustomed to having the run of the shop.

Specialization will also reduce the department's dependence on specific personnel. Although this may be interpreted as a loss of job security for individuals, it is a benefit for the organization as a whole. The loss of a key individual in the organization for some length of time due to vacation, illness, or the individual's leaving the company should not cause the organization extreme hardship.

New environment—new functional requirements

Specialization may imply that only one person is responsible for a specific function. To a large part this is true; however, backup support must be considered when planning the organizational structure of MIS for the new environment. The new environment will also generate new functional requirements. These new functional requirements may be due to the particularities of the new environment or the result of a transition to a large systems environment. In any case a new or revised functional organization will be required for MIS.

The demands of a new, large systems environment will call for the dedication of people resources, formalized methods and procedures, and the delegation of responsibility and authority. Managing the new environment will require new techniques and considerable assistance. Smaller shops, accustomed to a single manager directly responsible for and very actively involved in the entire MIS organization and its day-to-day functions, will find that a distribution of management responsibility will be required to adequately manage the new environment. Even MIS organizations that have already divided management responsibility may find that reorganization is required, further distributing responsibility and authority.

A model organization for the large systems environment

The functional organization model presented (see Figure 5.4.) is an example of a typical large systems organizational environment. Organizational structures such as this are currently in use in many large MIS organizations throughout the country. More importantly, this type of organization structure has proved to work very well for the large systems environment.

The primary objectives of this recommended organizational structure are:

Aligning the duties and responsibilities to a generally accepted organization structure

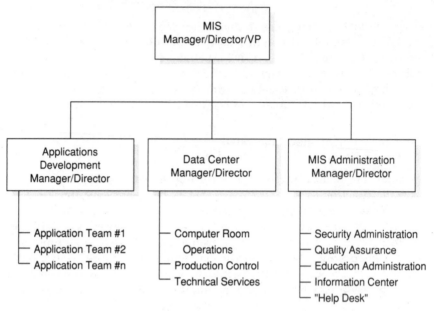

Figure 5.4   A model MIS organization for the large data-processing facility.

Providing for better separation of duties and responsibilities

Providing user personnel with a single source for assistance and problem resolution

Eliminating duplication of activities and responsibilities

Transfering noncomputer operation functions to other personnel, allowing computer operators to concentrate strictly on production processing and throughput

Developing an MIS organization that is more responsive to user departments

The overall organization is divided into three separate areas, each responsible for a specific set of specialized functions. The data center, applications development, and MIS administration comprise the MIS functional organization.

The heart of the organization is the data center. The data center is the production facility within MIS. All job execution responsibilities are focused within this group. The data center is normally composed of computer room operations, production control, and technical services. Computer room operations is responsible for the operation of the physical equipment and communications network. Production control's responsibilities include job scheduling, input/output control, and report distribution. If a centralized data-entry function is defined for the organization, it also resides with this group. Production control also acts as the direct-user interface for the data center. Technical services provides the data center with systems software support, network support, and operations support. Although technical services does provide support for the entire MIS organization, its primary function is to support the production facility. Technical services is responsible for the installation, implementation, and maintenance of the operating system and communication network as well as related support software products.

Applications development is responsible for the development, implementation, and support of all application systems and software. Their support responsibilities are limited to clearly identified application system issues at the system design and program level. This means that application development personnel should not be directly involved in front-line support of users or operations. Application development personnel are also end users themselves and must be recognized as such by the entire MIS organization.

MIS administration is a group that is not typically found in smaller organizations. In a large systems environment, it is essential for proper organization and control. MIS administration supplies required functions which need to be independent of the other groups as well as departmentwide functions which need to be centrally controlled. The typical MIS administration area is responsible for MIS security, quality assurance, and education administration. The information center is also usually a component of this organization, providing end-user computing support and nontechnical database administration support such as maintaining and controlling data dictionaries. The help desk facility also belongs to MIS administration. The help desk should function as a centralized facility chartered to provide the first line of support for the user community and the MIS organization itself. Clerical support for the system management functions of problem, change, and configuration management are also usually provided by help desk personnel.

The MIS administration group is a collection of several functions, some already in existence, moved from the data center operations area, and other new functions added to support the complexity of the new environment. The following responsibilities should be consolidated into this separate group:

Change management

Problem management

Configuration management

Quality assurance

Standards and procedures administration

Corporate data security administration

End-user computing support (including microcomputer systems support

Data base administration (nontechnical)

Training and education administration

These functions, if currently supported, are usually found spread over the entire MIS organization. In some cases direct responsibility for a given function may be unclear or the function may be performed by an individual as a spare-time project. The availability of spare time while developing a whole new environment, as in a conversion, is quite rare.

In the typical large systems environment these functions are performed by as many as five different functional areas within an MIS administration group:

Quality assurance

Security administration

Help desk

Info center

Education administration

In some large MIS organizations, the info center has expanded to where it functions as a separate group or department, particularly in shops with large database systems or extensive end-user computing.

Staffing the new environment

Staffing the new environment will present several problems. Most MIS organizations tend to use a phased or migration approach to conversions. This is a relatively safe approach because the existing staff does not have to immediately face the burden and pressure of supporting a full-blown production environment. Applications are gradually moved to the new environment, providing the staff with ample time to become acquainted with the new environment and learn their new or modified roles.

The phased approach does, however, have its drawbacks. For a considerable period of time during the conversion process two environments must be supported, the old or current environment and the new, target environment. This will more than likely require additional staff.

As applications are implemented in the new environment production workload requirements in the old environment will diminish. However, there is a certain amount of support overhead in the current environment that cannot be reduced at the same rate. The ability to reduce support personnel is dependent on more than the number of converted programs. For example, in a data center that runs a three-shift computer room operation a shift cannot necessarily be eliminated because some percentage of the application workload has been moved to the new environment.

When moving all production work at one time, as in the mass, or as it is more commonly known, the big bang approach, duplicate staffing is not an issue. Staffing problems will still exist, however, because existing personnel, inexperienced in the new environment, will not be able to function at the same levels of proficiency as they do in the current environment.

The need for specialization in adapting to the new environment may also create requirements for additional staff. The conversion project itself will require dedicated resources. Few organizations can spare existing personnel for any significant length of time and yet maintain production schedules and normal application maintenance requirements.

For some period of time additional staffing will be required. Organizations deal with these staffing issues in number of creative ways. Most will enlist the aid of temporary help during the conversion project. Others will hire additional permanent staff; some will do both. In any case this project, a corporate business decision, should not be shortchanged. Less-than-adequate resources will produce less-than-adequate results.

Aside from the staffing numbers issues, existing personnel must also be migrated to the new environment. It cannot be readily assumed that all individuals can simply read a manual and begin to function adequately in their new roles. Education and training will be required. A learning curve will exist for all personnel, and different people will require different levels of attention.

One company dealt with both the additional staffing requirements and training issues by adding three new permanent staff members. These three people were already experienced in an environment similar to the one toward which the company was moving. The first was an experienced application analyst, the next a senior computer operator, and the third a system programmer. The new staff members were assigned as team leaders for the conversion project. Their responsibilities included training existing staff.

Temporary help was also used to supplement the old environment rather than the new. Existing staff, experts in the current or old environment, easily directed the temporary help through normal production operations. The current staff was then freed to some extent of their day-to-day responsibilities and were able to concentrate on learning the new environment.

At the completion of the conversion project, all staff members were able to adequately support the new environment. The temporary help was gradually dismissed as the workload of the old environment diminished. The three additional staff members, hired earlier in the conversion project, left the organization of their own will shortly after the conversion was completed. All three had assumed, because of their knowledge and experience with the new environment, they would be placed in positions of authority after the project was completed. MIS management, however, made no such promises and remained loyal to the existing staff, viewing the conversion as a temporary project. The three new staff members were not satisfied with their new roles when assimilated into the normal organization. At the end of the conversion project, roughly a yearlong effort, the net change to MIS staff remained zero.

Education and training

A training and education plan must be prepared for the conversion project. This plan should identify training and education requirements for management as well as the entire MIS organization. Possible resources for training and education must be researched and examined to determine which method of education is appropriate for specific types of personnel (i.e., computer operators require a different level and type of training from programmers).

In some cases educational opportunities are limited for specific areas within the MIS department. In most cases, however, a number of methods are available and multiple vendors exist for providing education. Some of the more popular education and training possibilities are formal classroom training, self-study courses, computer-based training (CBT), and on-the-job training (OJT). A number of hardware and software firms offer education in areas of data processing from performance to DASD management. These courses must be carefully evaluated because vendors tend to present solutions based upon products they also market.

Formal classroom education is usually the best possible method of education. It provides the student with the opportunity to get away from the daily routine and focus attention on learning. Instructors are usually professional educators, not only knowledgeable in the subject matter but also well-versed in transferring their knowledge to the students. However, formal classroom training is generally more costly and usually inconvenient because of class schedules and locations.

Self-study courses are lower in cost, but require a considerable amount of self-discipline on the part of the student. On-the-job training is usually effective only when conducted by someone who is both knowledgeable and experienced in that particular area. OJT has proven to be particularly effective for operations personnel when guided by experienced operators.

A combination of different methods may be appropriate and cost-effective. For example, self-study courses can be used to provide basic education and classroom training can be used to reinforce or complement the self-study course. The resulting training and education plan should consist of an education program and schedule for each group within the MIS organization that identifies recommended resources and time frames. Class rosters cannot be developed until project teams are identified and assigned during the conversion project. As a general rule training and education should be provided as closely as possible to the students' planned use or need for the knowledge. For education to be effective it should be immediately followed by practice. This practice allows students to directly relate the knowledge gained in the classroom to their specific jobs, reinforcing the lessons learned.

A custom educational program composed of classroom work, designed specifically for the needs of the MIS organization, is the recommended approach to education for the new environment. This classroom-type education should consist of lectures and workshops. The combination of learning theory and then applying it in workshops will reinforce the knowledge acquired. The custom design of this type of education will allow all required topics to be covered in an accelerated, cost-effective manner. This type of class can also be held in-house, keeping expenses usually associated with classroom-type training to a minimum. Individual classes can be specifically tailored for operations and development personnel. A class of this type normally requires approximately two weeks to complete. A subset of this type of class is also appropriate for management, reduced to about one or two days. A number of vendors of educational services also supply this form of education.

The coordination of educational activities and resources within the MIS organization is essential to an effective education program. MIS educational programs must be scheduled and continually modified to remain current in the rapidly changing data-processing industry. It is also imperative that educational programs are tracked and evaluated to determine their effectiveness. Educational progress must also be monitored for all personnel, particularly when self-study courses are used extensively. The establishment of a continuing in-house training program for further personnel development is not necessarily a required part of the conversion project. It can be established as a separate project using the experience gained during the conversion. It is recommended, however, that an education administrator be appointed within the MIS organization during the conversion. This function is not necessarily a full-time requirement, but care must be taken to ensure that proper priority is placed on the functional requirements. This function should also be positioned in the MIS administration area.

User education requirements during the conversion process should not be overlooked. Actual requirements will vary depending on the severity of the environment change. Most users will require at least a minimum of training even if the environment change from their prospective is minimal. It is recommended that this training be coordinated by the assigned conversion project manager and considered during conversion planning. Additional end-user education related to application-system differences should also be planned with the conversion project. Application development personnel responsible for the particular systems or packages, or a training function separate from MIS education administration should be responsible for coordinating this form of educational requirement.

Chapter

6

Postconversion

Readjustment

If you've come this far in the book and have a good general understanding of the guidelines set forth, then you are ready for the final
activities. The preparation for the end of the conversion project and
the subsequent phase-down and project wrap-up sessions are planned
events in the overall project schedule. Once completed the conversion project quickly becomes past history. The project teams return
to their normal work assignments and there is a tendency toward
what is known as the "postconversion letdown." This will be evident
in project team members who have difficulty getting back to their
normal, slower-paced activities. The attitude may quickly shift to
"OK, we're here, now what?" The conversion probably caused a
major disruption to the shop's normal activities and many other
projects were put on hold. It's now time to restart those projects and
keep the shop activity at a high level using the new standards in
the new environment.

The same project-management methodology used for the conversion should be transferred into each new or existing project. When
the project team members leave the project they should be put on
other projects and not just resume the preconversion mode of work.
By keeping the conversion-project momentum going, the staff can
maintain the high project-productivity effort for a long period of time.

Eventually this higher productivity will become the normal work activity but will remain at a higher level than before the conversion.

The chart in Figure 6.1. shows the effect of the project on the normal workload and the opportunity for keeping the momentum going after the project is completed. The normal preconversion work activities are shown increasing with time as growth or other factors put pressure on the staff to do more. When the conversion project begins to build in activity the normal workload decreases accordingly. As the conversion project nears completion there is a rapid drop-off of project activity as the project personnel are phased back into their normal activities. There is a tendency for the resumption of normal work to slowly build back up to preconversion levels as the staff goes through the postconversion letdown. It is desirable to use the momentum of the project to make the resumption of normal work activities build up faster by using the personnel coming off the project to immediately start new or other projects. This change in slope and the difference between the high-productivity-work curve and the normal-work-resumption curve can be called the *momentum factor.* It represents the potential improvement in productivity that can be achieved if the project momentum is transferred to the normal workload.

At the successful completion of the project the users may ask when they are going to realize the benefits of the new environment. It will take skill, patience, and persuasion to convince the user community that the real payback comes over time as the newly gained capabil-

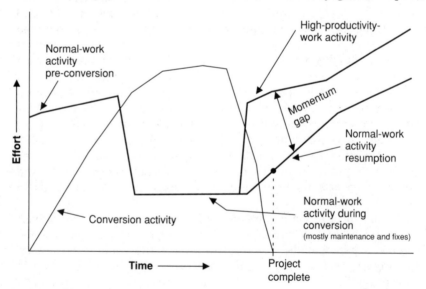

Figure 6.1 Momentum after the conversion.

ity becomes reality. The end-user community should notice a new attitude from their MIS counterparts. With proper training, as mentioned in earlier chapters, MIS personnel should quickly realize the increased efficiency and better control of the new environment. With better standards and working procedures, coupled with the proper training in using the new system, program developers will now have the ability to deliver quality projects to the users.

The initial justification for the project had both business and technical goals that were to be achieved with the conversion. As a part of the postconversion activities, time should be allocated to review what the goals were and whether the project achieved them or not. This review should involve the end users in order to correctly assess what goals were met. A successful conversion will meet most, if not all, of the goals and objectives (at least those that were not changed or modified). If a major conversion goal was 2-second response time and there is now 10-second response time, then something went wrong. A careful analysis should be made of all the objectives that are not fully met and plans made to resolve these problems. These analyses may yield other projects that were not known when the initial project for conversion was planned. As the project progressed, there may have been areas that were discovered as "opportunity projects" that have a high payback if developed.

If the conversion was from DOS to MVS, new responsibilities and functions have been created in MIS, including the possibility of an organizational change to meet these new challenges. With MVS, it is also possible to manage levels of service to the user community and meet performance objectives agreed upon by the users and MIS. MIS can measure machine performance and adjust internal parameters to optimize the job streams and data flow through the system and networks. Selection of the proper system software can further enhance the machine's performance levels by measuring selected system parameters that serve as indicators of that performance.

Of course not all conversions are major operating system changes. They could be major hardware changes or major database changes. Whatever the reason for the conversion, there will be major positive changes that will take place and newer levels of service achievable from the new environment. In major database changes, the reasons for converting are usually the need to provide a larger database capacity, more efficient use of corporate data, faster data-retrieval capability, better reporting capabilities, and more effective application development. In major hardware conversions going from one vendor to another, there might be significant changes to the operation of the shop as well as changes to the way the company will perform its business operations. Hopefully, the changes are not traumatic to the user community as far as disruptions are concerned, but there is major improvement to the way their business requirements are met. Their interface and view of the new system, as well as their trust in the capability of the new system to meet their future needs as the business grows, must be greatly enhanced.

After the conversion the new system will begin to support the business in the manner in which it was justified. Business growth in each department that is supported by MIS in turn leads to growth of the enterprise. MIS is a contributing factor to that enterprise and will begin to realize payback with the new environment by more effective and efficient operations. The increased support levels that should now be possible will be reflected in a more aware and effective customer base as the new capabilities are demonstrated and customer satisfaction grows.

The role of the MIS department will shift into the information-services mode of operation. The traditional view of management information systems as the folks who run the computers and write the software is too narrow in today's rapidly changing technical environment. The merging of voice, data, electronic images, and video into a single, integrated system (ISDN—*Integrated Service Digital Networks*) represents a major change in the way information is being handled in today's corporations. The new MIS organization is more globally defined and encompasses all aspects of information handling, including data communications, user-to-user communications, office automation, personal computers, and integrated digital voice/data networks, in addition to the traditional role. The newer technology being sold in the marketplace today presents the business community with countless choices on how to solve any manner of data-processing problems. It can be done better, faster, and less expensively than ever before and it is the mission of the new management information services department to act as consultants to their users and guide them through the technological thicket.

Even advertising is being directed at end users, and they are becoming more educated on the capabilities of the newer technologies. To keep the corporate computing resources developing in the most efficient direction, MIS must play the major role in supporting all the new technologies such as voice mail, electronic mail, fax, word processing, end-user computing, and all other new developments that hit the market daily.

MIS will evolve from being a collection of technical generalists, knowing all about the old environment and how to get jobs through, to that of being specialists. These specialists will be more skilled in meeting user needs and more familiar with their business requirements. Also, they will be specialists in the newer technology and able to offer solutions from a total system viewpoint, whether PC-based or mainframe-based. The most important change will be the removal of the dichotomy that has traditionally existed between users and MIS personnel which resulted from the technician trying to explain technical matters to uneducated users.

This relationship will shift to more of a partnership between MIS and the user, with MIS working closely with the user to help in problem solving. This partnership role will cause MIS to become more of a peer with the user, serving as a consultant to help the user in meeting needs in the most efficient manner.

With some of the newer software available that rapidly develops applications in a more simplified and efficient manner, there is less need for complex technical methods and ways of manipulating data in order to solve the application requirements. Effort can now be specifically directed toward a solution to a business problem in common business terms rather than working on the technical manipulation of moving, storing, printing, and sorting of the data elements required in the solution.

This new partnership between MIS and the user community will lead to greater productivity and more efficient usage of the new computational resources by generating a new spirit of cooperation between management information services and each business unit within the corporation. The mood will shift from "us vs. them" to "us vs. the problem."

The Real Conversion Payback

The real payback of the conversion will sometimes be more gradual and not a sudden, dramatic change. An additional role of the new management information services department will be to promote the new system in as favorable a light as possible. It doesn't hurt to keep selling the system after the conversion. If you had started a MIS department newsletter on conversion events, keep it going after the conversion is over. Soon enough the benefits will be recognized through better support, quicker response time, shorter job turnaround times, increased user satisfaction, and a more dependable resource.

Going through a major conversion may also help the MIS department eliminate many of the out-of-date systems and streamline the operation. Taking inventories of preconversion libraries can be very traumatic in some of the larger, more established shops that have been developing systems in-house for a long time. The inventory task may seem impossible, but with hard work and dedicated teams it can be done. By getting rid of these old, out-of-date, and unknown systems, the new environment will become more efficient with better control of the resource achieved by operating personnel.

With operational efficiencies there will be better support levels achieved. Better support levels mean that newer systems the users need to support their expanding operations will become reality. Growth is stressful to the corporate structure, but nowhere is it felt more than in the computational resource. Modern corporations heavily depend on computers for their information processing. With the new system in place, that dependency will become greater. It behooves the MIS group to achieve levels of service that meet and support the challenges of corporate growth. If the users perceive that MIS can support their needs, they will shift their concerns to solving their business needs rather than compromising them due to ineffective computer systems.

This does not mean that there are no limits to what can be achieved, or that there are not limits to the personnel resources developing systems. By removing one of the major concerns (resource limits) from the user groups by converting to more effective systems, their problem solution capabilities can be channeled to their specific needs. In the past, too much had to be sacrificed because of limitations on the hardware and software. Now, with the newer technologies, most of the technical limitations have disappeared. Only the budget for the newer equipment and additional personnel seems to be the major limit in today's growing corporate environments.

As new systems are developed on the target environment, your MIS department will have the ability to make contracts with the users to deliver guaranteed and specified levels of service. This may mean a specific turnaround time for month-end closing, or specific response times at the terminals. Whichever it is the MIS manager will be able to maintain and support the system so that it can meet these levels.

As the shop moves toward the data center approach to operations, MIS may want to explore user chargeback systems to understand the breakdown of usage of the resource. Service availability (up-time) and usage (work) become the foundation of support agreements. User chargeback can give MIS a dynamic measurement of who uses the resource, for how long, and for what time periods during the day. Besides service levels, this is important for budgetary purposes as you go before corporate management to justify the computational facility's projected budget. By showing usage factors, and demonstrating how they will meet the service levels, it will greatly help the end-user managers understand the relationship of their department's dependency to the corporate computational resource.

The Nontechnical Benefits

Other than financial and technical benefits to conversions, there are several quantifiable and nonquantifiable gains to be made. The main benefit is that the shop will have kept pace with the new technology, which makes the system personnel feel more like they are in the mainstream of computer knowledge. This will lead to more dedicated workers as they endeavor to learn and keep up with the new technology. As personnel grow proficient in the new system because of the effectiveness of the environment, the workplace becomes more efficient. Applications are usually easier to develop using newer techniques such as rapid prototyping in a 4GL (such as FOCUS), or high-powered editors.

Becoming more effective in system development with more efficient personnel will tend to slow down the staff growth rate in MIS. With the older technology, more people may have been needed to develop the systems that the users required on outdated and inefficient resources. Now with more effective methods available to develop these jobs, as well as more productivity per person, the need for new staff may decrease. There will always be room for talented, qualified people in the growth company, but the rate at which they are needed should slow down.

During growth periods the new environment will have the added benefit of attracting more qualified individuals to the staff. The managers will have a better selection and can choose the best person for each opening. Normally with the older system it was hard to find applicants with the outdated skills needed, so compromises were made in the selection that ultimately affected the productivity. Moreover, it was difficult to train personnel on the operation of some of the more custom systems, especially if the software was extremely outdated.

While it appears that all is positive, MIS management as well as corporate user management have the obligation to make all the beneficial things happen after the conversion. First, management must be supportive of changes in the organization that match the new environmental functions and responsibilities. In the MVS setting, there are significant differences in operations that must be addressed. No longer do operators schedule and run jobs; that becomes the function of production control. There are packaged solutions that automate the scheduling and restarting of job streams. If after converting to MVS nothing changes in the organization to meet these new responsibilities, then it will operate like a DOS shop and never meet the expectations of both MIS and the corporation's user community. This is a very key concept. You cannot run an MVS machine like a DOS machine and still gain all of the MVS benefits. Another major function may be to name a database administrator (DBA) to be in charge of the corporate database.

Moving into the new system may also affect some of the existing staff who are not comfortable with training and having to learn the new environment. This will sometimes weed out nonproductive members, but may also cause some of the productive members who have been with the organization a long time to leave. This can be averted if the proper approach is taken with the older staff members before the conversion by getting them involved in the conversion effort, even if it is just asking their opinion. Getting rid of unproductive employees could turn out to be a hidden problem rather than a benefit if the member has a contract or is vested. A better approach would be to move them into areas that are more suited to their talents. If that is impossible, then the only recourse may be to let them go. Care must always be taken in adverse personnel actions regarding the individual's position both formally and informally, their longevity with the company, and the potential unstabilizing effect on the remaining staff members.

The ultimate goal of the converted system should be to allow the users to think of the computational facility as a utility. It's there for their support and is dependable. An analogy that fits this case is the power company. We never really think of what electricity is, or how it's generated and distributed, we just flip the wall switch and expect the lamp to turn on. On the down side, when it's not on we get extremely impatient. Service disruptions can be minimized by proper recovery, restart procedures, and backup power sources.

As a utility function, the user community will be able meet their business objectives as their computational requirements are met with the new environment. In turn, user management is satisfied with the support level of the resource and will involve MIS management more in long-range business plans. MIS management will be viewed as a "can do" organization, capable of meeting goals and deadlines. Your motto should be "we can deliver."

The Emerald City

In the *Wizard of Oz* the Yellow Brick Road leads to success—the Emerald City. The path is often fraught with snares and detours, even wicked witches bent on the destruction of the mission. Eventually Dorothy and her friends make it. Likewise, the "Yellow Brick Road" for the conversion is also fraught with snares and detours, wicked witches and others, bent on seeing the project fail (see Figure

6.2.). Through it all, you and the project team must not lose sight of the goals of the conversion. It will be hard work—frustrating and nerve wracking—but good planning, good project discipline, and dedicated teamwork will save the day.

With the growth of the new technologies and the placement of resources in the hands of the users, the development process will increase exponentially. The multiplier effect across the company's user base by giving them ready access to the resource, and training them in the ability to use the resource to solve the problem, is astronomical. Companies that succeed in the future will also succeed in tailoring their resources to do this. A look at today's successful cor-

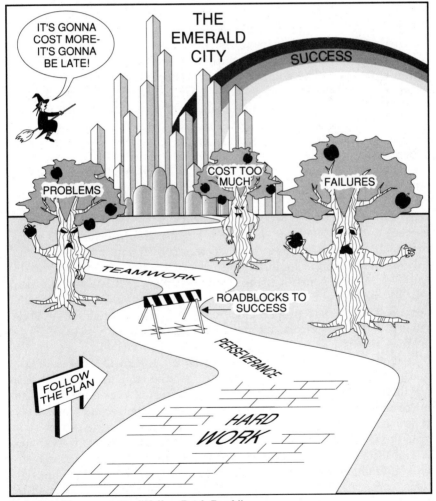

Figure 6.2 The conversion "Yellow Brick Road."

porations will show that they have found the balance between user involvement in solving their own problems and the computer department solving their problems for them. It's a matter of degree of involvement in the solution, or as one investor puts it, he likes to have his partners "put some skin in the deal." By involving and helping the users in the solution of their own problems, the company can be assured of the best possible outcome.

The benefits of working as partners with the end users cannot be overemphasized. Rather than discouraging users and acting as roadblocks, MIS can now be their champions as they work together with the users to solve the critical problems of the business. The information center approach, whereby users and MIS members meet and discuss their needs jointly, may not work for all shops. But it certainly should be a goal to have a user steering committee help set the goals for MIS productivity. As the users get more involved with MIS, and vice versa, an appreciation of each other's problems and limits will occur. The ebb and flow of systems and data will become a synergistic process, whereby the entire resource becomes greater than the sum of its individual parts. Optimization occurs on the highest level and not with the smallest element. Efficiencies are realized on total system operation for the good of all, rather than suboptimized for the few at the cost of the many.

Getting the resources and help to do a conversion is hard, but is only a part of the total picture. A major conversion puts a strain on the entire company. Outside help can alleviate some of the strain on the staff and prevent the organization from having to develop conversion experts. However, to ensure success the internal MIS organization, *you*, must be a part of the conversion process. If the conversion is simple and straightforward enough, then you should consider doing it yourself using the project plan. If it is complex, then outside help might be needed; but that help should not be totally depended upon. The proper amount of project-management involvement and the proper checks and balances need to be put in place to achieve success.

Is it worth all the effort? Is it worth all the cost? The rationale and justification were noble enough to get the support needed. If it's a failure due to uncontrollable factors you can always start over and make the necessary changes to ensure success the second time. Only time can answer the worthiness of it all. Most certainly without it growth would be slowed, if not stopped. Remember that a conversion is a positioning process that causes the company to accept new business challenges and new goals. As competition develops newer systems, corporations must keep up or fall by the wayside. The road to excellence is narrow and demanding. Using the full power of your computer resource is essential for a streamlined and efficient corporation. Being unable to develop the right systems at the right time to support the expansion of the business will lead to a stalemate of that growth. Conversely, being able to meet increasing customer demands, support rapid growth, and streamlining the operation of the company will all lead to the success that was paid for by the effort. Someday, in the twenty-first century, the manager will just switch on the computer like a light bulb to begin the corporation's day.

Conversion Case Studies

Rather than providing you with one in-depth conversion case study, which you may or may not relate to, several case studies are offered representing a cross-section of industry and embodying some of the more prevalent conversion business issues.

Please note that in all cases an outside partner was selected to assist in the conversion effort. It is a rare organization that has the specific technical skill-mix and the accompanying project management and planning expertise to successfully execute their own conversion without exorbitant drains on time, money, and resources.

Manufacturing

Company profile. A major U.S. manufacturer and marketer of pharmaceuticals for an international chemical company.

Business objective. Increase divisional control over corporate computing. Move all commercial business applications from the parent company service bureau and establish an in-house data center.

Constraints. Limited internal resources, physical space restrictions, and almost immediately after the completion date was set, they realized that they would need to move this date up by several weeks in order to meet year-end manufacturing and processing requirements.

Conversion specifics. High-level planning for the conversion began. As the enormity of the undertaking and the complexities of converting from one system architecture to another became apparent, the client selected an outside consulting firm as partner for the conversion effort.

The consulting firm began with an exhaustive inventory of the existing applications, precisely determining the relationship among all programs, files, and subroutines. After this close analysis, the consulting firm recommended that approximately 10 percent of their programs be replaced with packaged software in the new environment and five percent be redesigned for the new system rather than converted, and the remaining 85 percent would be converted.

A comprehensive conversion work plan was then drawn up that included both management and technical responsibilities and provided a realistic time frame based on project priorities, development schedules, programming resources, and installation of the new hardware. After a pilot conversion of the database software, the technical feasibility of the project was assured.

At this point the need to move the schedule up to meet year-end commitments became apparent. It was decided that additional resources would be required to assure that the new deadline would be met.

Since the additional labor force was not available internally, the conversion partner responded by providing several additional on-site consultants at the project's peak.

Since there was a shortage of actual physical working space, makeshift facilities for the additional staff were created adjacent to the data center that allowed the project to continue without disruption. The consultants were able to move the project through package preparation, translation, testing, and parallel production phases swiftly and efficiently. Being able to successfully freeze the systems during the conversion eliminated most of the complex control problems normally associated with such an undertaking, and the additional personnel allowed them to complete the conversion within the allotted time.

Resulting business benefits. The goal of migrating all commercial business applications from the old service bureau environment to a new in-house data center was successfully achieved. The long-term payoffs were improved MIS response to changes (additions or problems) within the processing environment. There was also an improved capability to respond to mechanization within the physical production departments. Finally they gained definitive control of computing capabilities and information system flow within their organization.

Utility

Company profile. One of 12 regional data centers for a multibillion dollar international energy company.

Business objective. A strategic information technology decision was made to ultimately align all 12 data centers under a single hardware vendor to facilitate vendor maintenance and support and increase interregional communications.

Constraints. The primary constraint was the complexity and sheer logistics of tackling a project this formidable. For this one data center, the conversion would ultimately affect over 2500 application programs, 50 systems, and 1.75 million lines of code, and would take four years to complete.

Conversion specifics. The first task was to build another computer room to house the new equipment. All preparations, plans, construction, wiring, flooring, and air-conditioning were completed within six months.

Simultaneously, policies and procedures were set up for each stage of the conversion, with special attention paid to quality control. An internal management team was put in place to handle the conversion and coordinate the outside vendors.

Their first action was to bring in a specialized conversion consulting company to manage the conversion itself. They in turn brought in the project-management skills and the conversion software that would allow them to reduce as much as possible the manual effort required to convert.

The project involved the re-creation of over 1000 databases. While most companies strive to make the technological changes throughout the conversion appear transparent to their users groups and keep disruption to a minimum, in this case the users were bound to be affected by a project of this magnitude. Special equipment purchased to provide increased performance strategically benefitted the users by easing the culture shock of working with the new system.

In order to keep the technical problems manageable, the strategy for the conversion was to approach it on a phase basis. The phased approach might cause some additional work but it would ensure against a system failure. The consultants identified every unit and cataloged them by size and complexity so that effort estimates could be provided for each unit of software converted.

This kind of planning for each phase of the project and meticulous attention to detail would ultimately enforce a structured approach throughout the conversion effort. It would also allow flexibility to respond to sudden business demands, changes in strategy, and even unexpected resource and budgetary constraints.

Resulting business benefits. Although all the data centers have not yet converted, it appears that the cost savings from consolidating fragmentary units and converting to state-of-the-art technology may well be passed on to the consumer in the form of reduced rates, uniform billing, and expanded services.

Internally, knowing that the conversion was feasible, time frames could be kept stable, milestones could be met, and with a custom workplan in place, two totally divergent firms worked as a seasoned unit to ensure a timely and successful project completion.

This has been a tremendous relief to the remaining data centers preparing to convert.

Transportation

Company profile. A national, over-the-road trucking firm that had experienced heavy growth during the previous three years.

Business objective. The results of an independent MIS-department requirements study substantiated the need for major improvements in current application systems and overall computing capacity just to keep up with the department's tremendous growth. To support long-range MIS department needs new hardware and an operating environment were recommended to replace the current system, which had reached capacity and could not be upgraded.

Constraints. Sufficient technical resources were not available through the MIS staff. Personnel knowledgeable in both the current operating environment as well as the selected target environment were especially scarce. It was necessary to complete the conversion in the allocated six-month time frame.

Conversion specifics. The first order of business was the development of a comprehensive implementation, education, and training plan. New technology was being implemented, and that would require a sharp learning curve. The initial choice was to solicit assistance from the new hardware vendor, but cost and other considerations dictated a different approach. To fill the resource gap, management authorized retaining the services of an outside consulting firm.

After an in-depth evaluation of their methodology, a firm specializing in conversions was retained to help manage, support, and execute the conversion within the allocated time. They performed a detailed study of the current environment and produced a workable plan for a timely completion of the project.

A help desk was set up to augment the internal education efforts and to assist the MIS department staff understand and adapt to the new technologies. When the consulting firm departed, the in-house personnel had to function as well in the new environment as they had in the old, without any loss of support to the users groups.

The consulting firm brought to the table an automated tool kit to support conversion of data processing entities, support of team activities, and verification of conversion results—the latter being a yardstick by which to measure the success of their efforts.

Strenuous project management, quality control, and tracking procedures were put into place. Conversion packages, or units of related programs, were assigned to follow-through teams that would be responsible for translation, compilation, testing, etc., of that package through final turnover of the converted programs.

It was decided that this follow-through team strategy would ensure better transfer of knowledge from the consultants to the company's staff, rather than assigning a different group of people to handle each conversion phase like translation or testing. This team approach also ensured better quality control and closer attention to detail.

Most of the conversion activities were completed well ahead of schedule. This was the result of three key factors. First, the people assigned to this project were of a high technical caliber. Next, a viable workplan and excellent methodology were followed. Finally, working relationships among the vendor, consultants, and permanent staff were outstanding. There was rarely a gap in communication.

Resulting business benefits. The company now has an entirely new technical platform that will allow them to keep pace with their business growth. They are better positioned, competitively, in their industry and are well positioned to meet their five-year business plan of diversifying through acquisitions.

Distribution and Service

Company profile. A large, retail-builders' supply firm serving the northeast corridor.

Business objective. Meet corporate demands for greater capacity and capitalize on their vendor's reduced maintenance fee program.

Constraints. In order to take advantage of their vendor's reduced maintenance-fee program, they would need to run a project parallel to the conversion. This project would include development of comprehensive standards and procedures, reviewing and updating problem management, configuration management, security, and disaster recovery. This parallel project was expected to cause a considerable drain on all resources.

Conversion specifics. The decision was made to convert. Not having any previous experience with conversions no one was sure what steps to take, what tools were available, the relative magnitude of the job ahead of them, or how to manage it. Consulting a sister company who had recently completed a successful conversion, they were pointed to an outside consulting firm for their solution.

They knew they wanted a local company they could develop a partnership with, a company with previous experience doing conversions as well as providing data-center management services, and a company that would allow them to participate in the project. Having found the consulting firm that satisfied their criteria, they were ready to dig in.

The consulting group sent in two teams. One prepared to set up appropriate standards and procedures to satisfy their vendor, and another team started the actual conversion effort. The project was separated into three major groups: 1) pilot systems, 2) inventory and distribution systems which had to be implemented together and 3) the remaining systems which could be implemented independently.

The project was staffed jointly by the company and the consulting firm. Most of the in-house staff was dedicated to the conversion project, while the remaining staff supported existing systems. All outside personnel worked solely on the conversion project. Management and planning for the conversion was shared by both companies. Each company had the day-to-day management responsibility for their respective staffs.

Automated conversion tools were used whenever possible to reduce the manual effort and increase the standardization of the converted systems. Planing was done in the beginning to identify any complexities that existed. A conversion technical guide was developed, which outlined the project, identified the complexities, and standardized solutions to those complexities. Throughout the conversion, an ongoing log was maintained of the problems they encountered and their solutions.

Effort estimates and schedules are initially prepared for each phase of the conversion and then modified as needed based on experience gained in each phase. The conversion technical guide was also continually updated to reflect that experience.

A relatively small system was selected as a pilot system to verify the proposed approach and tools. Since the new hardware and software had not yet been installed, conversion and testing of the pilot system was done at the consulting company's off-site facility. The pilot also allowed the new environment to be established and verified before the user groups became dependent on it.

Once the conversion approach and tools were tested and verified, the pilot served as a guideline for converting the remaining systems.

Resulting business benefits. The outcome was a successful project, completed within the time frames and budgets established for it. The first major group of systems (inventory and distribution) were implemented on schedule. The remaining systems were completed prior to the original deadlines established for the conversion. The standards and procedures were developed and implemented with time to spare to satisfy their vendor's requirements for qualification in the maintenance-fee reduction program.

Insurance

Company profile. Health claims subsidiary of nationwide insurance company.

Business objective. The foremost consideration in deciding to allow the lease to expire on their current hardware and bring in an entirely new vendor was to increase service. They wanted to speed the processing of claim payments for their policy holders.

Constraints. As with most companies that have decided to bring in a completely new system, the current staff was totally unfamiliar with the intricacies of what their new environment would be. They anticipated a strenuous learning curve for both the management and technical staffs.

Conversion specifics. Realizing that the day-to-day business operations must continue without disruption of service to their policy holders, the current staff was quickly split into teams. One team was solely responsible for maintaining their current systems, one was assigned exclusively to supporting the actual conversion, and a floating team assisted both sides of the house when peak load demands were high.

Although new people and new skills could have been brought in to support the new technology, management was committed to keeping the continuity and cohesiveness of their current staff intact. An outside consulting firm was utilized to provide the very specialized skills necessary to ensure the success of the project, but their staff still had to be trained.

Although training was ongoing throughout the conversion project, it was deemed critical that at least part of the staff become proficient in the new environment as quickly as possible. It was decided that the floaters would be the first team to start intensive training for the new environment (as the conversion project wound down, this would also be the first team assigned to actually start working with the new technology). As members of this team completed training, members of the other two teams were freed to start their own level of training.

On a staggered basis throughout the 10-month conversion effort, all staff members received the required training without unduly impacting either maintenance of their current systems or conversion to the new environment.

Staff morale remained high because everyone felt like a contributor to the success of the project and no one felt left behind in the wake of the new technology.

Outside consulting companies were evaluated not only for their conversion expertise and management ability, but almost as importantly for their corporate personality and business ethics. The more closely a firm's management attitudes, business ethics, and service approach to their customers was aligned with their own attitudes and ethics the better the partnership and the more likely the success of the conversion.

Ultimately, their new hardware vendor was the one that recommended the consulting firm that was later selected. As an added plus, the consulting firm had staff training built in to the methodology they employed—realizing their client's need to be immediately productive in the new environment.

Because company management fully supported the conversion, and was capable of making necessary decisions quickly and knowledgeably—whether it was an increase in the operating budget, or running three shifts instead of two for the duration of the project, or approving acquisition of peripheral equipment—the conversion itself was a dénouement, coming off smoothly, efficiently, and within original time and budget.

This particular short-term partnership was so successful that permanent staff positions were offered to several individuals from the consulting firm.

Business benefits. The original goal of speeding up the claims-processing cycle was achieved. In the long run, the real benefit was to the policy holders, whose premiums weren't (incidentally) increased to fund the million-dollar project. In fact, their premiums were still at the same rate almost one-and-a-half years after completing the conversion.

Glossary

APPLICATION A business function that has been automated so that end users access the computer system or its output to perform the function.

BATCH PROCESSING Computer processing in which programs or jobs are grouped together and submitted to the mainframe processor as a unit.

BENCHMARK A baseline trial test designed to examine the quality or effectiveness of the new system environment. Similar to **PILOT TEST**.

BIG BANG Term used to describe the migration technique of moving all applications to the target environment at a single point in time. Opposite of a phased-in approach.

CAPACITY SIZING To determine the total required processing power or size of a processor that is needed to handle a given amount of computing workload.

CHANGE CONTROL A procedure for documenting all changes to source programs (e.g., modifications or enhancements) after the conversion process is initiated. Controlling this process ensures that the final converted system reflects program changes.

CICS IBM's on-line telecommunications monitor.

CODE GENERATOR A tool for producing a new program code quickly and in conformance with predefined standards, program structures, naming conventions, etc.

COMPLEXITY ANALYSIS The process of determining those peculiarities of the inventory that may pose technical difficulties during the conversion execution. Examples include dissimilar source and target languages, data formats, or batch vs. on-line processing.

CONFIGURATION A logical combination of computer programs and data that are packaged together and treated as a distinct unit for purposes of conversion.

CONFIGURATION MANAGEMENT The formal logging and tracking of reported problems designed to ensure that problems are resolved in a reasonable timeframe.

CONTENT INTEGRITY An assessment conducted during scanning of the conversion inventory to determine the quality of the data in the source environment and whether that data is being used as indicated.

CPM Acronym for Critical Path Method, a planning methodology which identifies the minimum amount of time and the associated tasks required to complete a project.

CPU   Central Processing Unit. The component of a hardware configuration which performs the data manipulation and analysis. Usually synonymous with *mainframe.*

CRITICAL PATH   The longest path (minimum time) through the tasks of a project from start to project completion.

CUTOVER   The process or point in time when the old (source) environment or system is discontinued and the new (target) system becomes operational.

DASD   Direct Access Storage Device. A peripheral hardware device used for storing and accessing large amounts of data.

DATA BRIDGING   Term used to describe the process of migrating data from a nonconverted application to a converted application and vice versa.

DATA CENTER   The production facility within MIS responsible for job execution. Typically includes computer-room operations, production control, and technical services.

DATA CONVERSION   Modifying data only so that it may be ready for the target environment.

DELIVERABLE   A manageable and measurable parcel of work used in determining progress status.

DOS   One of IBM's operation systems. Usually found on midrange installations.

END-USER COMMUNITY   Those individuals within the organization who will directly access the computer system or who will make substantial use of the output from the system.

ENTITY   A unit of the system that is part of the total inventory or part of the package to be converted. Includes programs, files, procedures, etc.

EXPERT SYSTEMS   Automated tools which ask a series of questions in order to provide the best possible answer to a complex question.

FILE COMPARATOR   An automated tool for comparing the data output from a test run to ensure that the test results from the source and target systems are identical.

FUNCTIONAL EQUIVALENCE   The condition that results when the functionality of the source application is duplicated in the target application. Usually refers to the perspective of the end users rather than the data-processing technicians.

FUNCTIONAL TRANSPARENCY   The condition that results when the functionality of the source system is identical in the target system as viewed from the end user who is accessing and utilizing the system.

IMPLEMENTATION   The final phase of conversion. This includes the activities of parallel testing (if possible) and production turnover.

INVENTORY   That set of entities (programs, data, etc.) that comprises the source system and are targeted for conversion.

LANGUAGE EXTENSIONS   Modifications made by a data center to a vendor-supplied programming language to enhance or improve its capabilities. These extensions may represent especially difficult problems during a conversion.

LEXICAL SCANNER   A program which searches source code or other text for words or specified character strings for counting purposes.

LOT   Synonymous with **PACKAGE**.

MAPPING   The process of assembling information gathered from inventory scanning into a logical, tabular format. The main objective is to identify what programs, files, or job streams are related to each other. Similar to cross-referencing.

MAP/IMAP   IBM's marketing assistance program that provides third-party assistance for IBM client's for conversion, software development, etc.

MILESTONE   Term used to identify a point in time which serves to measure or evaluate progress in a project. It may also involve a key decision or a point when several activities must culminate.

MIPS   Million Instructions Per Second, term used to gauge the central processor's speed and capacity.

MIS   Management Information Systems, a common term used to identify the organizational department responsible for systems design, programming, and computer operations.

MVS   One of IBM's operating systems. Usually found on medium to large installations.

NETWORK   A graphic representation of all tasks and their relationship regarding a specific project.

ON-LINE PROCESSING   Computer processing usually performed interactively by end users directly connected through terminals to the processor.

OPERATING SYSTEM   The set of software that operates the high-level functions of the computer such as scheduling the processing and managing the peripheral devices (e.g., printer, disk storage units).

PACKAGE   A group of logically related computer programs and data that are packaged together and treated as a distinct unit for purposes of conversion.

PARALLEL TESTING   A testing activity where the newly converted system is monitored against the system to ensure complete integrity before the new system is officially put into production and the old system is discontinued.

PARSING SCANNER   A program that can provide data and instruction chaining statistics from a review of source code.

PERIPHERAL DEVICES   The hardware or equipment that is attached to the central processing unit. Includes disk drives, tape drives, printers, terminals, communications controllers, etc.

PHASED-IN   Term used to describe the migration technique of moving applications to the target environment as they are converted. Opposite of a big bang approach.

PILOT   A small subset of the applications library which is used first for testing then as the initial phase to be converted.

POPULATED   Loading a database or file with information for the first time.

PROBLEM MANAGEMENT   The formal logging and tracking of reported problems designed to ensure that problems are resolved in a reasonable timeframe.

QUALITY ASSURANCE   The management, administration, and enforcement of predefined procedures and standards within the MIS organization.

REDEVELOPMENT   The process of extracting system requirements from the old (source) system and developing a whole new set of programs and systems.

REPLACEMENT   The process of obtaining and installing new or qualitatively better software package to serve in place of the old (source) software package.

REWRITE   Basically a transliteration of existing programs into the new environment without changing the logic of the system or modifying the code. Although this process can be performed rather rapidly, the operation of the new system is somewhat unpredictable.

SCOPE CHANGE   An unexpected or unanticipated change in the nature of volume of work to be accomplished during the conversion.

SEMANTIC CONVERSION   Changing applications in terms of the deeper meaning of the functions and services that are provided to end users.

SOURCE PROFILE   The process of identifying the special characteristics of the source inventory. This assists in analyzing complexities to be expected during conversion.

SQL   System Query Language. Used to access a relational database.

STEADY STATE   Term used to describe a gradual conversion of application programs. Related to *phase, kernel, lots,* and *packages.*

TECHNICAL GUIDE   A document developed for each conversion that describes the technical procedures needed to accomplish the technical tasks. Also presents solutions to the technical complexities identified in the planning phase.

TOOL   A set of automated processes that are designed to accomplish conversion activities (e.g., program code translation, data/file transfer) more efficiently or accurately than if done manually.

TRANSACTION   A measurable unit of work. Includes the steps of entering data, processing by the CPU, and receipt of the results by the user.

TRANSLATION   The process of changing one version of program code or a language into another version or language so there is minimal change in logic or functionality.

WORKBENCH   A comprehensive set of *tools* or software intended to fully automate the conversion process. The workbench executes the conversion in a rigid way with less opportunity for ad hoc intervention.

Index

Index